UNIT B

THE CHANGING EARTH

Theme: Models

GET READY TO

OBSERVE & QUESTION

How do volcanic eruptions affect Earth?

This beautiful sunset occurred after a volcanic eruption in the Philippines. How might a volcano erupting in the Philippines affect other places on Earth?

EXPERIMENT & HYPOTHESIZE

How are earthquakes located and measured?

Create your own mini-earthquake and then record the tremor. Later, find out how you can locate the epicenter of an earthquake.

INVESTIGATE!

RESEARCH & ANALYZE

As you investigate, find out more from these books.

- ***Volcanoes and Earthquakes*** by Basil Booth (Silver Burdett Press, 1991). Besides learning all about volcanoes and earthquakes, you'll find out what fumaroles and hot springs are!

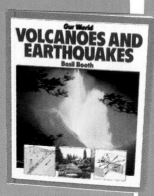

- ***Earthquake at Dawn*** by Kristiana Gregory (Harcourt Brace,1992). Daisy Valentine watches in horror as San Francisco is rocked by an earthquake in 1906.

- ***Surtsey: The Newest Place on Earth*** by Kathryn Lasky (Hyperion Books for Children, 1992). The wonderful photographs in Lasky's book take you on an adventurer's tour of a newly formed island.

WORK TOGETHER & SHARE IDEAS

Is an earthquake likely to occur where you live?

Working together, you'll have a chance to apply what you've learned. With your class you'll explore the geologic events of your state and town. You'll find out whether you're likely to experience an earthquake or a volcanic eruption. Finally, you'll find out how to prepare for these events.

CHAPTER 1

CRACKED CRUST

Beneath the oceans are the highest mountains and the deepest trenches on Earth. Here molten rock erupts along underwater mountain ranges. The eruptions are part of the constant change taking place on the ocean floor.

Mapping the Ocean Floor

Few will ever see firsthand the impressive mountains and valleys below the surface of the oceans. The best view has been through sonar maps produced by ocean-floor surveys done from ships.

Now scientists in California and New York have used satellite information to produce an improved map of the ocean floor. Radar equipment on the satellite measured the distance from the satellite to Earth's surface, providing a map of the surface of the oceans. But how does this help map the ocean floor?

Because of gravity, ocean water piles up around underwater mountain ranges. Less water is found over the deep trenches. This means that the surface of the ocean has hills and valleys that imitate the contours of the ocean floor. So a map of the *surface* of the ocean provides a picture of its *floor* at the same time. Why is it important to have an accurate map of the ocean floor?

Coming Up

◀ Improved maps show that the sea floor has features as varied as those on land.

DO CONTINENTS REALLY DRIFT ABOUT?

About 80 years ago, Alfred Wegener suggested that at one time all the continents were joined together in one large landmass known as Pangaea. Further, he suggested that the continents split apart and drifted to their current locations. Other scientists laughed at him. Could he have been right?

Activity

The Great Puzzle

Take a look at a map of the world. You may notice that the continents fit together like the pieces of a jigsaw puzzle. Can you reconstruct the "supercontinent" of Pangaea from today's continents?

MATERIALS

- scissors
- outline map of the continents
- sheet of paper
- glue
- map of the world
- *Science Notebook*

Procedure

1. Using scissors, cut out each of the continents from the outline map. Cut along the dark outlines.

2. Arrange the continents on a sheet of paper so that they all fit together, forming one super-continent.

3. After you have obtained your best fit, make a map by gluing the pieces onto the sheet of paper in the pattern that you obtained. Keep your map in your *Science Notebook*.

4. Use a map of the world to find the name of each continent on your map. Label the continents.

Step 1

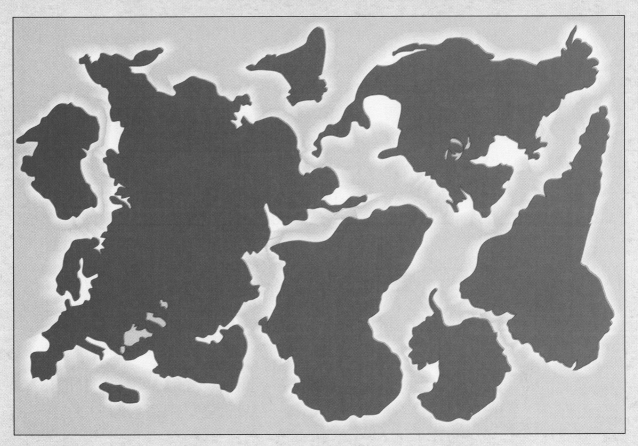

▲ Outline map of the continents

Analyze and Conclude

1. How well did the continents fit together to make a single supercontinent?

2. **Compare** the map that you made with one showing the present locations of the continents. What can you **infer** about Earth's continents if both maps are accurate?

3. In your reconstruction, what continents border on the continent of North America?

4. What evidence, besides the shapes of the continents, might scientists look for to confirm the idea that continents were once joined in a supercontinent?

INVESTIGATE FURTHER!

RESEARCH

Look in a world atlas, such as *Goode's World Atlas*, to find a map that shows Earth's landforms. Use this information to explain why Wegener thought Earth's landmasses were once joined as a supercontinent.

Alfred Wegener
and the Drifting Continents

The year was 1911. Nabisco introduced its cream-filled chocolate cookie called Oreo. Marie Curie won a Nobel Prize for her isolation of pure radium. The National Urban League was founded.

That same year, Alfred Wegener read a scientific paper that changed his life. The paper presented evidence that millions of years ago a land bridge may have connected South America with Africa. To Wegener the evidence suggested that the two continents were at one time a continuous landmass. Further, he thought that *all* of Earth's continents might once have been joined. But he dropped the idea when he couldn't explain how such vast landmasses had moved.

In 1912, Wegener gave a scientific talk about his ideas on moving continents. He suggested that the landmasses were once joined and had since drifted apart. Nearly all who attended the talk, as well as others in the scientific community, thought Wegener's idea was ridiculous. Wegener still held on to his hypothesis.

In 1915 he published a book explaining how Earth's continents and oceans might have formed and changed over time. His evidence came from many fields of science. Wegener noted that the continental shelves fit together like the pieces of a puzzle. A continental shelf is an underwater part of a continent that extends under shallow water from the edge of the land down to a steeper slope. He noted that the fossil remains of certain species of plants and animals were found on widely separated continents. The plants and animals that left these fossils could not have crossed the oceans.

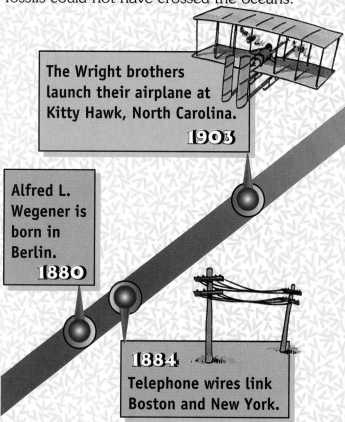

The Wright brothers launch their airplane at Kitty Hawk, North Carolina. **1903**

Alfred L. Wegener is born in Berlin. **1880**

1884 Telephone wires link Boston and New York.

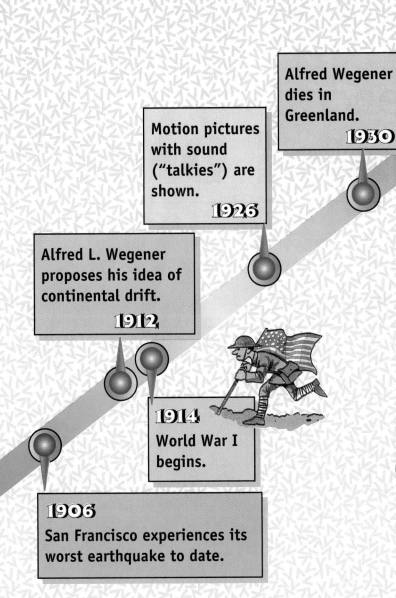

Alfred Wegener dies in Greenland. 1930

Motion pictures with sound ("talkies") are shown. 1926

1967 **Scientists show renewed interest in theory of continental drift. Today the idea is accepted.**

Alfred L. Wegener proposes his idea of continental drift. 1912

1914 **World War I begins.**

1906 **San Francisco experiences its worst earthquake to date.**

Finally, Wegener produced evidence that the climate of many parts of the world has changed dramatically over time.

Wegener used this evidence to reconstruct a supercontinent, **Pangaea** (pan-jē′ə), or "all land." Wegener hypothesized that this giant landmass existed about 200 million years ago. He proposed that over time the landmass broke apart, and he concluded that continents are still moving. Wegener's hypothesis on the movement of continents is called continental drift. Despite all the evidence cited, it wasn't until the 1960s that scientists took Wegener's hypothesis seriously. ■

200 million years ago

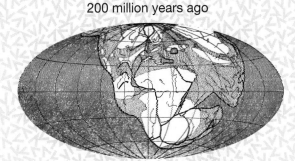

140 million years ago

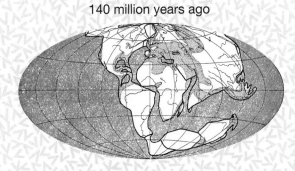

60 million years ago

▲ **Wegener's maps of drifting continents**

Evidence for
Continental Drift

Alfred Wegener was a meteorologist—a scientist who studies weather. But he was interested in many fields of science. His **theory of continental drift**, which stated that the continents were once one landmass that had broken apart and moved to their present positions, was supported by many lines of evidence.

One piece of evidence was the puzzle-like fit of continental shelves. Recall how you fitted the continents together on page B6. Wegener found that when he joined the continental shelves of Africa and South America, the fit was nearly perfect. Many of the rocks that made up mountains in Argentina were identical to those found in South Africa. It seemed unlikely to Wegener that these identical layers of rocks were formed in such widely separated places at the same time.

By the time Wegener had published the third edition of his book, he had found other similarities among certain rocks. He had discovered that diamond-rich rocks in South Africa were very similar to diamond-rich rocks in Brazil. Many of the coal beds in North America, Britain, and Belgium were deposited in the same geological period. And a thick red sandstone layer crossed continental boundaries from North America to Greenland, Britain, and Norway. Look at the map shown below. What pieces of evidence can you name that support the theory of continental drift?

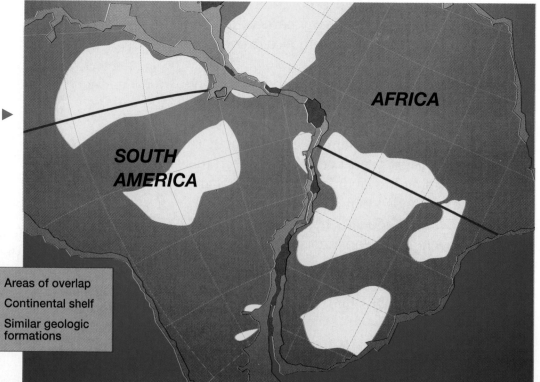

The fit of the continental shelves is evidence that South America and Africa were once joined. ▶

AFRICA

SOUTH AMERICA

■ Areas of overlap
■ Continental shelf
□ Similar geologic formations

Wegener also noted that certain fossils were preserved in rocks of the same age on different continents. He argued that the remains of these once-living organisms were so similar that they must have been left by the same kinds of organisms. One of these creatures was a small reptile called *Mesosaurus*, which lived its life in fresh water. Other fossils found in rocks that were very far apart were those of *Glossopteris*. Remains of this plant had been discovered in South America, Australia, India, and Africa. How, Wegener asked, could this plant have survived the different climates of these four landmasses?

Because of his training as a meteorologist, much of Wegener's evidence included information about climate. You probably already know that Earth can be divided into three major climate zones. The tropics are located near the equator and extend to about $23\frac{1}{2}°$ north and south of the equator. The temperate zones lie between the tropics and the polar zones. The polar climatic zones extend from about $66\frac{1}{2}°$ north and south to the poles.

Wegener noted that fossils of beech, maple, oak, poplar, ash, chestnut, and elm trees had been found on a small island named Spitsbergen, near the North

◄ A variety of *Glossopteris*, a plant with fossil remains found in widely separated continents.

Pole. These trees generally grow only in temperate areas. Today, however, the island is covered for much of the year with snow and ice because it has a very cold climate—a polar climate.

Coal forms in swampy marshes that receive a lot of rain each year. Today coal beds are forming in areas near the equator and in some temperate regions. Wegener proposed that coal beds in the eastern United States, Europe, and Siberia formed when the continents were joined and were located closer to the equator.

Another variety of *Glossopteris* ▼

Wegener used all of these different lines of evidence to reconstruct the supercontinent Pangaea. He hypothesized that this single landmass existed about 200 million years ago. Over time, he proposed, the landmass broke apart and the continents drifted to their present positions on Earth's surface. ■

◄ *Mesosaurus*. Fossil remains of this reptile were found on widely separated continents.

Continents on the Move

Wegener's hypothesis stated that Pangaea began to break apart about 180 million years ago. These smaller pieces of land drifted to their present position as Earth's continents. Although Wegener's idea was at first criticized, today it is accepted by scientists.

The maps on the next four pages show how landmasses—later Earth's continents—moved over time. Arrows on the continents show the direction in which they moved. Compare the location of the continents millions of years ago with their present location. ■

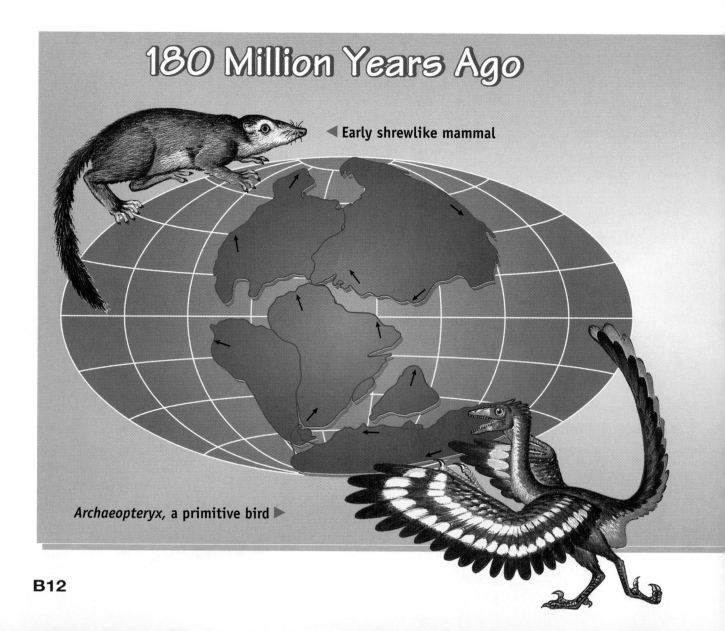

180 Million Years Ago

◄ Early shrewlike mammal

Archaeopteryx, a primitive bird ►

135 Million Years Ago

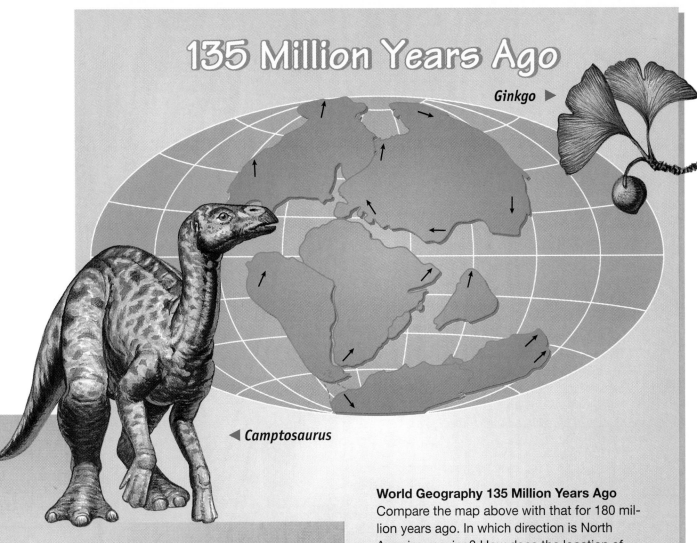

Ginkgo ▶

◀ *Camptosaurus*

World Geography 180 Million Years Ago
About 180 million years ago, North America, Europe, and much of Asia began to split from South America and Africa. India separated from the landmass around the South Pole and started moving northward. Australia and Antarctica drifted to the south and west. The Atlantic and Indian Oceans began to form.

Life About 180 Million Years Ago
Green algae, corals, and sponges lived in the warm waters that covered much of Earth. Ammonites, which looked like giant snails, also inhabited Earth's oceans. Many amphibians, including ancestors of modern frogs, roamed the land. The first dinosaurs appeared on Earth. Somewhat later, *Archaeopteryx*, a birdlike animal, also lived on Earth. Conifers were the dominant plants.

World Geography 135 Million Years Ago
Compare the map above with that for 180 million years ago. In which direction is North America moving? How does the location of India compare with that on the map for 180 million years ago? In which direction is Australia moving? What has happened to South America and Africa?

Life About 135 Million Years Ago
Sea urchins, sand dollars, and green algae populated the seas. Dinosaurs such as *Camptosaurus*, *Stegosaurus*, *Allosaurus*, and *Apatosaurus* roamed the land. Birds soared through the sky. Conifers, ferns, and ginkgoes made up the plant life on the planet.

65 Million Years Ago

World Geography 65 Million Years Ago

Although the map below shows Earth's landmasses 65 million years ago, it probably looks much more familiar to you than do the two maps on the previous pages. Describe how the locations of South America and Africa differ from their locations 135 million years ago. Describe the direction in which North America is moving. How far north has India moved as compared with its position 135 million years ago? Which two southern present-day continents are shown here still joined?

Life About 65 Million Years Ago

Fish, plankton, corals, and sponges were major forms of marine life. Insects were very abundant on land. These creatures pollinated the new flowering plants. *Ankylosaurus*, *Triceratops*, and *Tyrannosaurus* were some of the kinds of dinosaurs that lived at this time.

Ankylosaurus, **a heavily plated animal** ▶

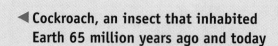

◀ **Cockroach, an insect that inhabited Earth 65 million years ago and today**

Today

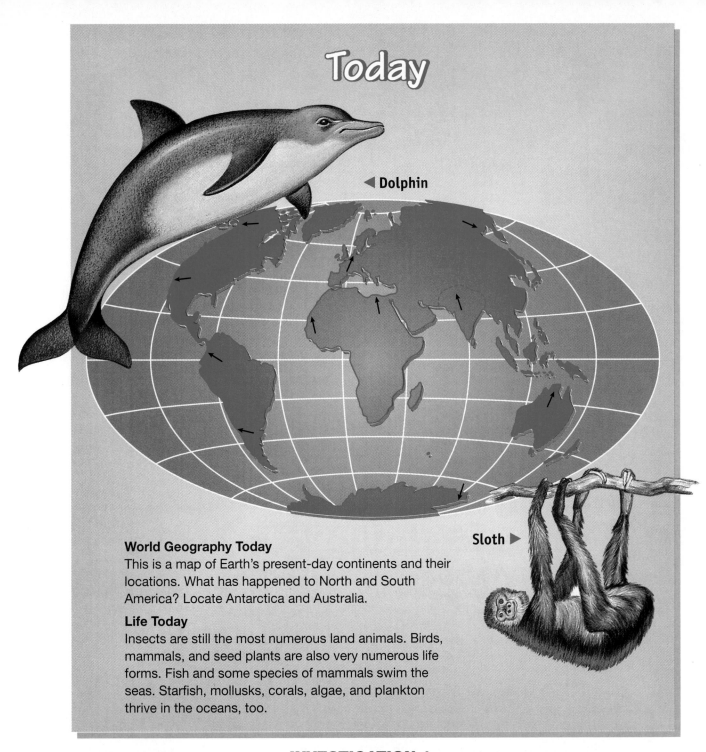

◀ **Dolphin**

Sloth ▶

World Geography Today

This is a map of Earth's present-day continents and their locations. What has happened to North and South America? Locate Antarctica and Australia.

Life Today

Insects are still the most numerous land animals. Birds, mammals, and seed plants are also very numerous life forms. Fish and some species of mammals swim the seas. Starfish, mollusks, corals, algae, and plankton thrive in the oceans, too.

INVESTIGATION 1

1. Evidence of glaciers has been found in many parts of southern Africa! What does this information tell you about the possible location of this continent at some time in the past?

2. Describe the kinds of evidence that Alfred Wegener and other scientists have used to show that the continents move over time.

WHAT DO THE LOCATIONS OF VOLCANOES AND EARTHQUAKES TELL US?

INVESTIGATION 2

Earthquakes and volcanoes make our world a bit shaky! Think of all the stories you have heard about earthquakes and volcanic eruptions. Can the locations of these events give us clues about continental drift?

Activity

Earth—Always Rockin' and Rollin'!

Did you ever wonder why earthquakes occur where they do? See if you can find any pattern in the locations of earthquakes.

MATERIALS
- earthquake map of Earth
- tracing paper
- *Science Notebook*

How is Earth like a cracked eggshell? ▼

Procedure

1. Study the earthquake map. Every dot on the map represents a place where a strong earthquake has occurred. Look for a pattern that the dots form. Describe this pattern in your *Science Notebook*. Discuss your observations with your team members.

2. On tracing paper, use your pencil to trace and then darken the pattern formed by the earthquake dots. Work with your team members to decide how to draw the pattern.

3. Think about the way a cracked eggshell looks. Earth's **crust**, which is its outermost, solid layer, is a lot like a cracked eggshell, broken up into large pieces. Look again at the pattern of the earthquake dots. How is the pattern of the dots like the cracks of an eggshell? Record your answer.

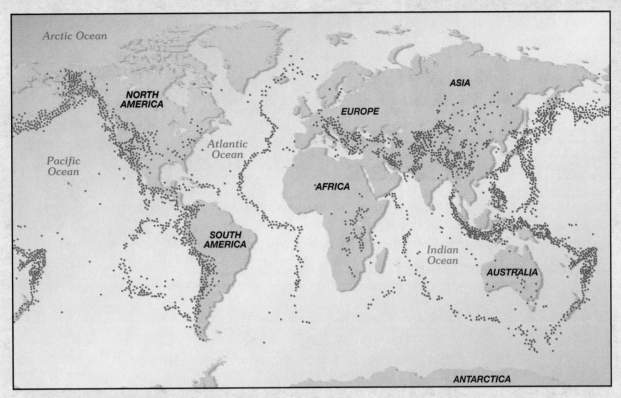

▲ **Earthquakes around the world**

Analyze and Conclude

1. Earth's crust is broken into large pieces called **tectonic plates**. Use your tracing and the map to locate some of these tectonic plates.

2. Earthquakes occur mostly along cracks in Earth's crust. Predict some locations where earthquakes are likely to occur. Record your predictions.

UNIT PROJECT LINK

Create a tectonic-plates map that shows your town. Also, show the tectonic plate(s) surrounding the plate that includes your town. How close is your town to the edge of a tectonic plate? Place a map pin where your town is located. Predict how likely your town is to have an earthquake.

As you go through this unit, collect data from news articles about earthquakes and volcanic activity around the world. Place map pins on a classroom map showing where this activity is taking place. Look for relationships between earthquakes, volcanoes, and tectonic plates.

Activity
Volcanoes and Earth's Plates

MATERIALS
- map of Earth's volcanoes
- map of Earth's earthquakes (page B17)
- *Science Notebook*

Earthquakes occur at the edges of huge slabs of crust and upper mantle called tectonic plates. *Are volcanoes and earthquakes found in the same places?*

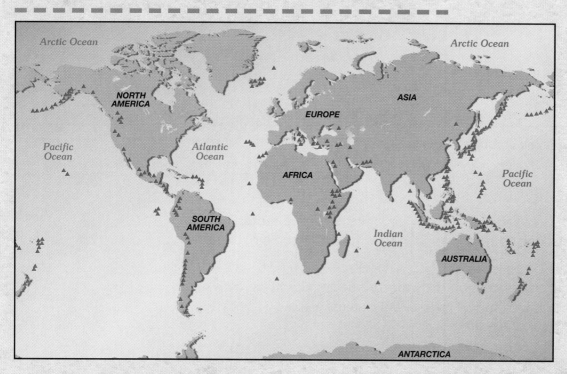

▲ Volcanic activity around the world

Procedure

Study the map of Earth's volcanoes and compare it with your map of Earth's earthquakes. In your *Science Notebook*, list the places where volcanoes occur.

Form a hypothesis about the locations of volcanoes, earthquakes, and the edges of Earth's tectonic plates. Record your hypothesis. Discuss your observations with your group.

Analyze and Conclude

1. Using the maps on B17 and B18, describe where both earthquakes and volcanoes occur.

2. How do the locations of earthquakes and volcanoes help identify Earth's tectonic plates?

The Cracked Crust:
Tectonic Plates

Floating Plates

Sometimes you'll hear the expression "It's as solid as a rock." This expression means that whatever is referred to is solid, permanent, and dependable. We may like to think that rock is solid and permanent, but even large slabs of rock move. Actually, nothing on the surface of Earth is permanent and unmoving. Even the continent of North America is moving. The movement is very slow, but it is movement, just the same. The slow movement of North America and the continents can be explained by the theory of plate tectonics.

In the late 1960s, scientists expanded Alfred Wegener's idea of drifting continents and proposed the **theory of plate tectonics**. The word *tectonics* refers to the forces causing the movement of Earth's rock formations and plates.

The theory of plate tectonics states that Earth's crust and upper mantle are broken into enormous slabs called **plates**, also called **tectonic plates**. (The **crust** is Earth's outermost, solid layer. The **mantle** is the layer of Earth between the crust and the core.) The continents are like enormous ships attached to these floating plates. Scientists think that currents, or slow plastic movements in the mantle, cause the plates to move across Earth's surface. The currents are caused by differences in temperature in Earth's interior regions.

This theory is one of the most important theories about Earth's geologic history. It has guided scientists in the way they think Earth might have looked millions of years ago. Plate tectonics has helped them reconstruct the ways the continents might have moved over millions of years.

A wedge showing Earth's layers (*left*); a section of the crust and upper mantle (*right*)

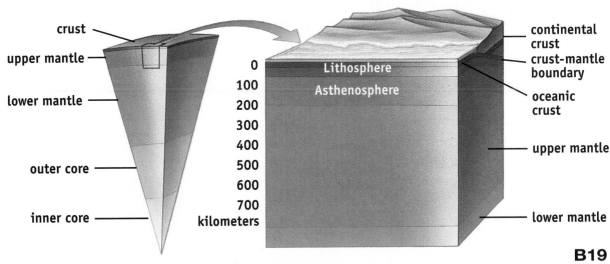

EARTH'S TECTONIC PLATES There are seven major plates and several minor ones. Many of the plates are named after the major landmasses that are parts of the plates. The plates act like rafts that carry Earth's crust and upper mantle around on a layer of semisolid material. Study the map shown to the right. You will see that most of the United States is located on the North American Plate. In what direction is this plate moving? In what direction is the Pacific Plate moving?

Makeup of the Plates

What do the tectonic plates consist of? Each plate is formed of a thin layer of crust, which overlies a region called the upper mantle. In a plate that carries a continent, the crust can be 40 to 48 km (25 to 30 mi) thick. In a plate that is under an ocean, the crust can be only 5 to 8 km (3 to 5 mi) thick. The drawing at the bottom of this page shows the makeup of a tectonic plate.

Interacting Plates

Plates can interact in three ways: (1) They can come together, (2) they can move apart, and (3) they can slide past one another. Places where plates interact are called **plate boundaries**. As you probably know by now, earthquakes and volcanoes occur along plate boundaries. In Chapter 2 you will find out much more about what happens along these boundaries. ■

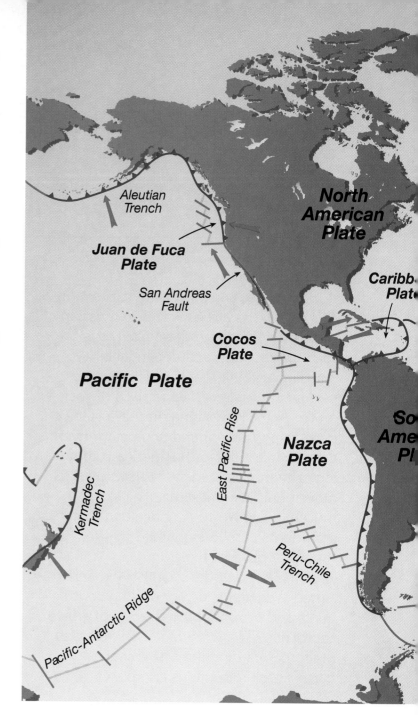

Tectonic plates can carry a continent, an ocean, or both a continent and an ocean. ▶

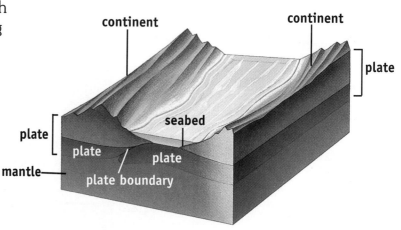

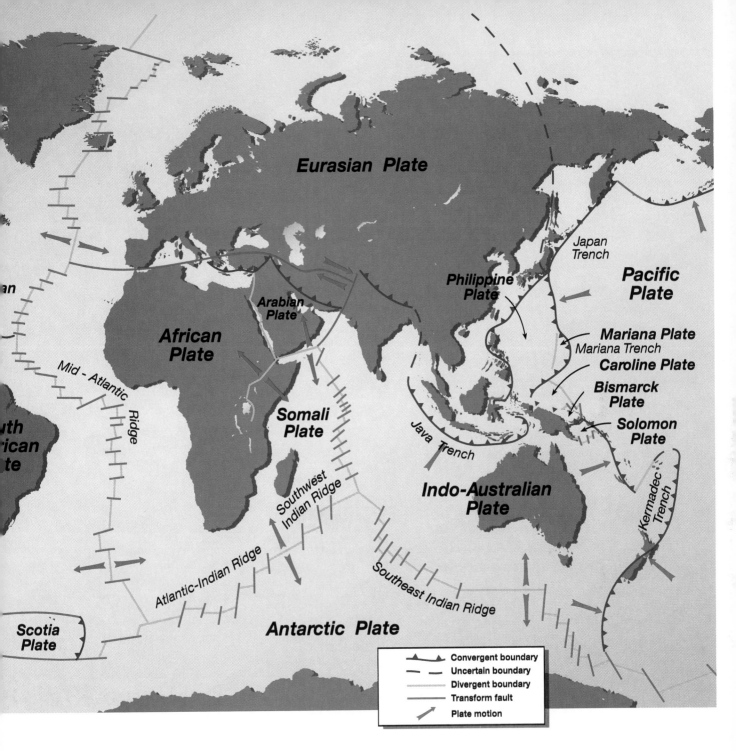

Eurasian Plate

Japan Trench

Pacific Plate

Philippine Plate

Mariana Plate
Mariana Trench

Caroline Plate

Bismarck Plate

Solomon Plate

Arabian Plate

African Plate

Mid - Atlantic Ridge

South African Plate

Somali Plate

Java Trench

Indo-Australian Plate

Southwest Indian Ridge

Kermadec Trench

Atlantic-Indian Ridge

Southeast Indian Ridge

Antarctic Plate

Scotia Plate

| Convergent boundary |
| Uncertain boundary |
| Divergent boundary |
| Transform fault |
| Plate motion |

INVESTIGATION 2

1. Predict what might happen in 10 million years to Los Angeles (on the Pacific Plate) and San Francisco (on the North American Plate) if the two plates carrying these cities continue to move in the direction in which they are now moving.

2. What is the connection between earthquakes, volcanoes, and tectonic plates? Give evidence to support your answer.

WHAT DOES THE SEA FLOOR TELL US ABOUT PLATE TECTONICS?

How do scientists know what the sea floor looks like? Is there evidence for plate tectonics hidden beneath the waters? Find out in this investigation.

Activity

Sea-Floor Spreading

New rock is being added to the sea floor all the time. Model this process in this activity.

MATERIALS

- sheet of paper with 3 slits, each 10 cm long
- 2 strips of notebook paper, each 9.5 × 27 cm long
- metric ruler
- scissors
- pencil
- *Science Notebook*

Procedure

Prepare a sheet of white paper as shown in the top drawing. Draw mountains. The middle slit represents a very long crack in the ocean floor, called a **mid-ocean ridge**.

Pull strips of notebook paper up through the middle slit and down through the side slits, as shown. These strips represent magma that is flowing up through the ocean ridge and then hardening. The strips are a model of the way the ocean floor spreads. This process is often called **sea-floor spreading**.

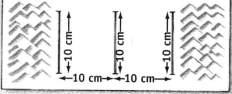

Analyze and Conclude

Consider that the magma coming up through the ridge is hardening into rock. What can you infer about the age of the rock along each side of the ridge? Record your ideas in your *Science Notebook*. Where do you think the oldest rock on the sea floor is?

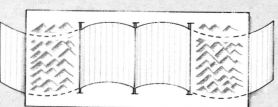

Activity

Building a Model of the Ocean Floor

The sea floor is much like the dry land. Tall mountains and deep valleys exist there. You can build your own model of these structures.

MATERIALS
- modeling clay
- shoebox with lid
- metric ruler
- grid
- pencil
- tape
- *Science Notebook*

- -

Procedure

1. Place modeling clay along the bottom of a shoebox until the clay is about 2.5 cm (1 in.) deep in all places.

2. Add enough clay to mold an underwater valley, mountain, and an uneven surface.

3. Tape the grid to the lid of the shoebox.

4. Use your pencil to punch holes in the grid and lid wherever there are small circles on the grid. Put the lid on the shoebox.

Analyze and Conclude

1. Which ocean floor features does your model illustrate? **Record** your answer in your *Science Notebook.*

2. How could someone determine the shape of the "ocean floor" without looking inside the shoebox?

INVESTIGATE FURTHER!

RESEARCH

Find out the height and extent of underwater mountains. Where are the highest underwater mountains? Are these mountains related in any way to Earth's plates?

Steps 2 and 4

Activity
Mapping the Ocean Floor

The water is too deep to swim through, and there's no light. So how do scientists figure out the shape of the ocean floor? Use the ocean floor structures that you built in the last activity to model one way scientists do it!

MATERIALS

- coffee stirrer
- fine-tip marker
- plastic straws
- scissors
- shoebox model of ocean floor, including grid taped to shoebox lid
- metric ruler
- *Science Notebook*

Procedure

1. Cut a coffee stirrer so that it is the same length as the height of the shoebox. Beginning at one end of the stirrer, mark each centimeter along its length.

2. The stirrer is a model for a sound beam from a ship's sonar system. After a ship's sonar transmits a "ping," it "hears" (receives and records) an echo from the ocean bottom a short time later. The length of time needed for the echo to return to the ship is related to the depth of the ocean at that point. Each hole in the grid on top of the shoebox represents the location on the surface of the ocean from which a ship's sonar has sent out a sound beam or "ping."

3. Locate hole *A1* on the grid taped to the shoebox lid. Place your stirrer into this hole, inserting the 1-cm end first. In your *Science Notebook,* set up a chart for recording the depth to the surface of the clay below each hole. **Record** the depth for the hole at *A1*. **Measure** and **record** the depth to the surface of the clay under each hole on the grid.

4. Cut a piece of straw to match the depth that you measured under each point on the grid. For example, if you measured a depth of 4 cm, cut a straw piece that is 4 cm long.

Hole	Depth (cm)
A1	
A2	
A3	
A4	

Hole	Depth (cm)
B1	
B2	
B3	
B4	

Hole	Depth (cm)
C1	
C2	
C3	
C4	

5. Now stick a piece of straw in the hole to match the depth you measured under that hole. For example, if you measured 4 cm at *A1*, stick a 4-cm straw into hole *A1*. Next, *push the piece of straw through the shoebox lid* so that the straw hangs down below the lid. Tape the top end of the straw in place so that it is even with the shoebox lid. Insert a length of straw in each hole on the grid until every hole has a straw hanging from it. These straws represent sonar beams that are sent down to the ocean bottom. What do you think the lid represents?

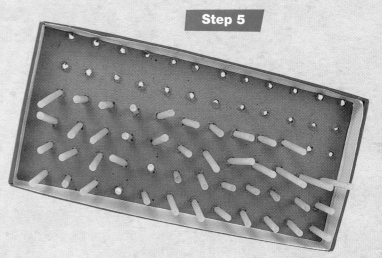

Step 5

Analyze and Conclude

1. Remove the lid, cut away one side of the shoebox, and replace the lid. Look at all the straws. How well does the pattern of the straws match the highs and lows of your ocean floor?

2. Would your straw model be more accurate if you had taken more depth readings? Why?

Analyze and Conclude, #1 ▼

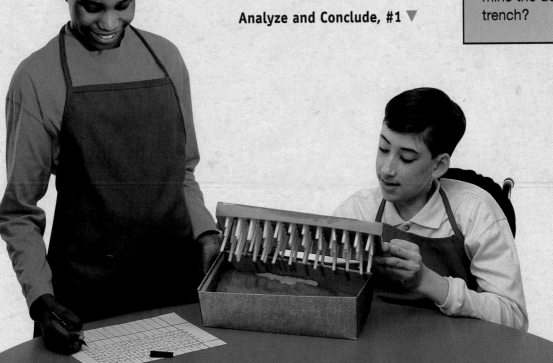

INVESTIGATE FURTHER!
. . . .
RESEARCH

Find out where the deepest ocean trench is located and how deep that trench is. How did oceanographers determine the depth of that trench?

Sonar:
Mapping the Sea Floor

Did you try the activity on pages B24 and B25? If you did, then you built a model of sonar—a method for finding the shape and depth of the ocean floor. *Sonar* stands for *so*und *na*vigation *a*nd *r*anging.

British naval scientists first developed sonar in 1921. During World War II (1939–1945), sonar was used to detect enemy submarines. Scientists realized that sound could be used to measure the distance from a ship on the surface of the water to the bottom of the ocean. A sonar device sends out a sound and then listens for an echo to return. By using sonar, scientists can measure the time between sending out a sound and receiving the echo of that sound. Then, by knowing this time and the speed at which sound travels through sea water,

they can compute the depth of the ocean at that point. In the activity "Mapping the Ocean Floor," the straws you pushed through each hole in the grid represented a sound impulse that might have been sent out by a ship carrying a sonar device.

As a ship with sonar moves along the surface of the ocean, it sends out frequent sound impulses. The sound impulses travel down through the sea water, strike the ocean floor, and then send back an echo. Each echo arrives at a receiver

1. Ship sending out signals from sonar device

2. Sound sent out by sonar device and returning echo

3. Sea floor

How sonar is used to map the sea floor ▶

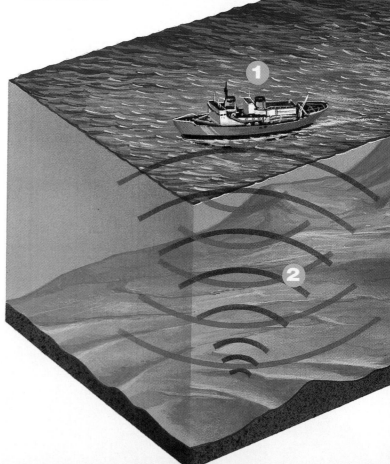

back at the ship and is recorded on a recording chart. The sonar device records the length of time required for the echo to return from the ocean floor. It then computes the depth of the ocean floor at that point. Finally, the depth is registered on a scale.

If the total time for a sound to travel from the ship to the ocean floor and back is 6.60 s, and sound travels through sea water at 1,530 m/s, the sound has traveled a total of 10,098 m. The distance from the ship to the ocean floor is half the total, or 5,049 m. By assembling all the measurements taken as the ship moves through the water, scientists can produce a map of a section of the

ocean floor. The more readings they take, the more accurate their map will be. Sonar has allowed scientists to discover many new features of the ocean floor. For example, they have found some places that are over 10,600 m (6.3 mi) deep. That's over 10 km! They also have found undersea mountains higher than Mount Everest, which is 8,848 m (29,028 ft) high!

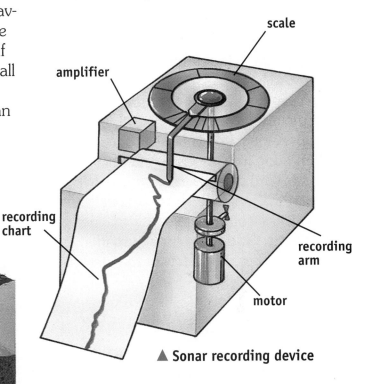

▲ Sonar recording device

Probing the Land with Sonar

Sonar can also be used on land. Sound pulses can be sent through the ground, and the returning echoes can be used to identify different layers of soil and rock as well as to locate deposits of natural gas and oil. ■

Magnetism
Tells a Story

You have probably used magnets many times. Perhaps you used one to pick up a string of paper clips or to hold notes on the refrigerator door. How is Earth like a magnet?

A magnet is an object that attracts certain metals, including iron, steel, and nickel. A magnet has two ends, or poles. When hung from a string, the pole that turns toward north is called the *north pole* of the magnet. The pole that points south is the *south pole* of the magnet. A **magnetic field** is the area around a magnet where the effects of magnetism are felt.

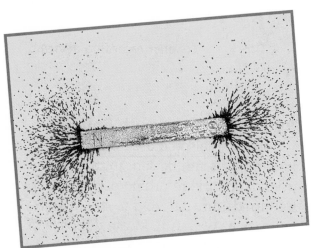

▲ **Iron filings show the magnetic field around a magnet.**

Earth is like a giant magnet, and it has two magnetic poles. These poles are inclined, or tilted, about 11° from the geographic poles. The magnetic field around Earth is thought to be due to movements within Earth's fluid outer core, which is composed mainly of iron and nickel. For reasons unknown, Earth's

▲ **The earth is like a giant magnet surrounded by a magnetic field.**

magnetic field reverses, or flips, from time to time. Such a change in the magnetic field is called a **magnetic reversal**.

At present, the magnetic field is said to be normal. This means that the north-seeking needle of a compass will point toward Earth's north magnetic pole. What do you think will happen when the field is reversed?

You probably know that some of Earth's rocks contain iron. When these rocks formed from magma, the particles in the iron lined up with the magnetic field of the time, much as a compass needle lines up with Earth's magnetic field. Scientists can use this lining up of iron particles to find the direction of Earth's magnetic field at the time the rock formed.

Scientists use a device called a magnetometer (mag nə täm'ət ər) to detect magnetic fields. This device can show how particles of iron line up within rock. Magnetometers have been used by oceanographers to study the magnetic fields of rock on the ocean floor. What the scientists found surprised them!

When the scientists studied the sea floor at mid-ocean ridges and on either side of the ridges, they found a magnetic pattern. There were long stretches of rock in which iron particles were lined up in one direction. Then there were other stretches of rock, parallel to the first, in which the iron particles lined up in the reverse direction. This pattern of reversals continued from the mid-ocean ridge outward, away from the ridge. A further

finding was that the pattern on one side of the ridge was exactly the same as the pattern on the other side of the ridge.

The drawing below helps explain the magnetic patterns on the ocean floor. At the center of the drawing is a mid-ocean ridge. Magma flows up from below the ridge and then hardens into rock on the sea floor. Only when iron-containing rock is fluid can the iron particles line up in a magnetic field. Once the rock hardens, the iron does not change its direction. The arrows show the magnetic directions of the iron in the rock at the mid-ocean ridge and on either side of the ridge. Note the repeating pattern.

Scientists have found that rocks closer to mid-ocean ridges are younger than rocks farther from the ridge. The magnetic patterns in the sea-floor rocks and the different ages of the rocks led scientists to a startling conclusion. New sea floor is continually being formed along underwater mountain chains, or mid-ocean ridges! As two plates separate along a ridge, magma fills the separation. As it is carried away from the ridge due

Sea-floor spreading. Magma bubbles up and flows out along the ridge. When it hardens, it forms rock. On either side of a mid-ocean ridge are layers of magnetized rock. Each arrow represents a magnetic reversal. ▼

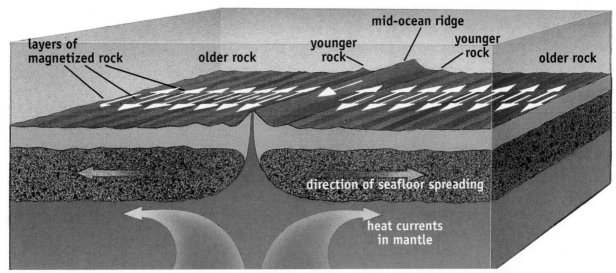

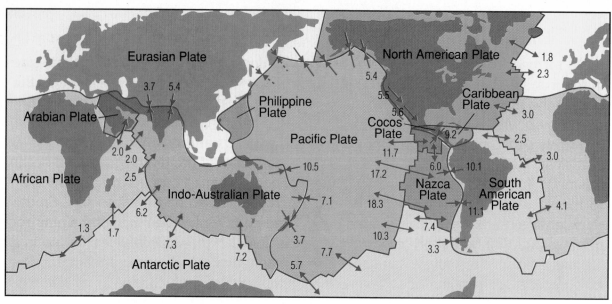

▲ **Map showing rates at which plates separate and move together. The rates are in centimeters per year.**

to convection currents in the mantle, the magma cools. As it cools, the iron in the magma lines up with Earth's magnetic field. This process by which new ocean floor is continually being added is called **sea-floor spreading**. Recall that you constructed a model of sea-floor spread-ing on page B22. Sea-floor spreading is strong evidence for the theory of plate tectonics.

Look at the map above that shows rates of sea-floor spreading along the Mid-Atlantic Ridge. Where is spreading the fastest? Where is it the slowest? ■

SCIENCE IN LITERATURE

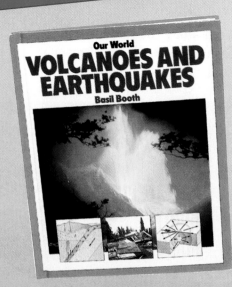

Our World
VOLCANOES AND EARTHQUAKES
Basil Booth

VOLCANOES AND EARTHQUAKES
by Basil Booth
Silver Burdett Press, 1991

What are some famous earthquakes? How is one volcanic eruption different from another? What makes a geyser, such as Old Faithful in Yellowstone Park, erupt like clock-work about every 65 minutes? You can look up the answers to these questions and more in *Volcanoes and Earthquakes* by Basil Booth.

The edges of tectonic plates can get pretty complicated. Find the San Andreas Fault on the big map on pages 14–15 of *Volcanoes and Earthquakes*. It looks like a straight line. Now look at the close-up map of the San Andreas Fault system. What might make it harder for scientists to predict the next earthquake in Los Angeles than it is to predict one in San Francisco?

Heating Up Iceland

GLOBAL views

In Iceland, some families don't need ovens to bake their bread; they simply place the dough inside a hole in the ground. Do they have underground ovens? Yes, but these ovens are created by natural processes taking place inside Earth. Below ground, but still close to the surface, there are very hot rocks. These rocks are heated by magma that bubbles up from deep inside Earth. Icelanders use these heated rocks to bake things in their underground ovens.

Helpful Shifting Plates

Movement of Earth's plates can cause trouble. Earthquakes and volcanic eruptions often occur along the edges of moving plates. But there are regions where plate movement can be helpful. In Iceland, for example, moving plates produce underground ovens that use an inexpensive kind of energy—geothermal energy.

Why It Is Hot

Iceland lies on the Mid-Atlantic Ridge, a chain of mountains running through the middle of the Atlantic Ocean. This small country is also located on the edge of two plates—the North American Plate and the Eurasian Plate. As these two plates move away from each other, hot

◄ **A geothermal plant in Iceland**

A geyser formed by the heating of water within Earth ▼

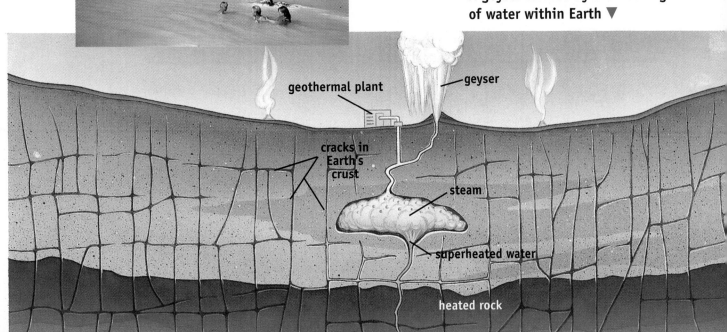

geothermal plant — geyser

cracks in Earth's crust

steam

superheated water

heated rock

magma rises up from inside Earth, heating the underground rock. The heated rock in turn heats any nearby ground water, changing it to steam. Some of this steam spurts out of the ground in the form of huge geysers.

Energy From Earth

Icelanders use this heated underground water as geothermal ("hot earth") energy. This energy, which comes from heat produced inside Earth, is used by the Icelanders to heat their homes, businesses, swimming pools, and greenhouses. The steam produced by the heated water runs generators that produce electrical energy.

Value of Geothermal Energy

Compared to other forms of energy, geothermal energy has many advantages, as you can see in the table below. Which form of energy is used where you live?

Geothermal energy is used now in several parts of the world besides Iceland—such as in Italy, Japan, Australia, New Zealand, Russia, and the United States. Some of the same processes that can lead to a volcanic eruption can also be turned to useful purposes. The use of geothermal energy in Iceland shows that processes inside Earth can provide people with the heat and electricity they need every day. ■

Comparison of Forms of Energy

Energy	Advantages	Disadvantages
Fossil fuels	no toxic waste	nonrenewable, polluting
Geothermal	less polluting than fossil fuels or nuclear energy	produces sulfur, boron, and ammonia wastes
Hydroelectric	cheap form of energy; renewable, nonpolluting	dams cause flooding of valuable land
Nuclear	cheap, renewable, powerful	toxic waste; risk of radiation leaks
Solar	renewable, nonpolluting	expensive development and maintenance

INVESTIGATION 3

1. You are planning a TV program about the mysteries at the bottom of the sea. How would you explain sea-floor spreading to your viewers?

2. Describe some of the most important features you might find along a mid-ocean ridge. Explain how these features are formed.

REFLECT & EVALUATE

WORD POWER

crust   Pangaea
mantle   plates
magnetic field
magnetic reversal
mid-ocean ridge
plate boundaries
sea-floor spreading
tectonic plates
theory of continental drift
theory of plate tectonics

On Your Own
Review the terms in the list. Then write one new thing you learned about each term.

With a Partner
Use the terms in the list to make a word-search puzzle. See if your partner can find the hidden terms and tell you what each one means.

BUILD YOUR PORTFOLIO

Write a story that tells what you would see if you were the pilot of a research submarine that dived around a mid-ocean ridge.

Analyze Information

The maps on pages B17 and B18 show the location of earthquakes and volcanoes. Why are there so many earthquakes and volcanoes located around the shores of the Pacific Ocean?

Assess Performance

The two strips of paper in the model on page B22 represent the spreading sea floor. Make a similar model and use it to show how magnetic reversals occur on each side of a mid-ocean ridge. Write an explanation of how your model shows what happens at mid-ocean ridges.

Problem Solving

1. Oceanographers have found a large mountain range that runs down the middle of the South Atlantic Ocean between Africa and South America. Careful measurements show that South America is moving away from Africa at about 3 to 5 cm each year. How would you explain this?

2. Explain how the same kinds of rock could be found in Norway, Scotland, and parts of eastern Canada and the eastern United States.

3. Dinosaur skeletons have been found in Antarctica, but they could not have lived in such a cold climate. How could they possibly be there?

CHAPTER 2

TECTONIC PLATES AND MOUNTAINS

The Himalayas, the Andes, and other great mountain ranges have existed for millions of years. The largest of all mountain ranges is actually beneath an ocean. How do mountains form? Do mountains on land and beneath the ocean form in the same way?

The Strangest Volcano

The West Antarctic ice sheet stretches for hundreds of kilometers across the continent of Antarctica. This seemingly unchanging land with its 1.6-km thick (1-mi thick) ice holds a secret that reminds us of how highly active Earth is.

Donald Blankenship and Robin Bell are both geophysicists (jē ō fiz'i sists), scientists who deal with Earth's weather, wind, earthquakes, and so forth. Blankenship and Bell were flying over the West Antarctic ice sheet when they noticed a caved-in area that measured 48 m deep and 6.4 km across. What could cause such a strange hole in the thick ice?

Using radar to see through the ice, the researchers discovered a 630-m mountain—a volcano. Imagine finding a volcano under a thick sheet of ice!

Coming Up

◄ Map showing presence of volcanic rock under the ice sheet.

WHY DO TECTONIC PLATES MOVE?

Wegener's hypothesis on continental drift helped to explain why the continents appear to be just so many pieces of a jigsaw puzzle. However, his hypothesis didn't explain why the continents moved. What force can move such huge plates of rock?

Activity
The Conveyor

Heat is a form of energy. Energy can do work. How can heat energy from Earth's interior move tectonic plates? In this activity you'll construct a model that shows what moves tectonic plates.

Procedure

1. Fill an aquarium with cold water.

2. Punch a 5-mm hole in the side of a milk carton, near the bottom. Punch another hole near the top of the carton.

3. Place a length of string over the hole near the bottom so that it extends down 2.5 cm below the hole. Cover the string and hole securely with a strip of duct tape, as shown.

4. Repeat step 3, this time covering the hole near the top of the carton.

MATERIALS

- aquarium
- cold water
- milk carton (0.24 L)
- 2 lengths of string (60 cm)
- duct tape
- measuring cup
- hot water
- food coloring
- scissors
- metric ruler
- paper towels
- *Science Notebook*

Step 3

5. Using a measuring cup, fill the milk carton with hot water colored with food coloring. Seal the carton with duct tape.

6. Place the carton in the middle of the aquarium. Predict what will happen when the holes in the carton are opened. Record your predictions in your *Science Notebook*.

7. Have a group member hold down the milk carton while you carefully pull the strings to peel the tape off the holes. Watch what happens. Record your observations.

8. Form a hypothesis on how the movement in the aquarium is a model of the movement of material in Earth's crust and upper mantle. Discuss your hypothesis with your group.

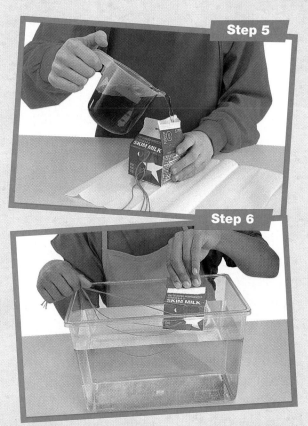

Analyze and Conclude

1. What happened in step 7 when you removed the tape from the holes?

2. Did the hot water do what you predicted it would do? Compare your predictions with what actually happened.

3. If the hot and cold water represent the layer of Earth known as the mantle, which is just below the crust, how might the mantle move tectonic plates?

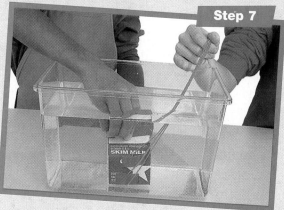

INVESTIGATE FURTHER!

EXPERIMENT

Predict what would happen if you floated a small piece of paper directly over the milk carton before you opened the holes. Then try it and compare your prediction with what actually happened.

Moving Plates

Recall from Chapter 1 that Earth's crust and upper mantle are broken into seven large slabs and several small ones. The slabs are called tectonic plates. These plates move over Earth's surface an average of several centimeters a year. Just what keeps these enormous slabs in motion?

Tectonic plates make up a part of Earth called the lithosphere. The word part *litho-* means "rock." You probably know that *sphere* means "ball."

The **lithosphere** (lith'ō sfir), then, is the solid, rocky layer of Earth. It is about 100 km (62 mi) thick. This part of Earth includes the crust, with the oceans and continents, and the rigid uppermost part of the mantle.

Have you ever slowly pulled on some silicon putty? What happened to the putty as the result of the force you applied? It stretched, didn't it? Suppose you gave the putty a quick, sharp tug. What would happen? The putty would snap and break. What do these two activities tell you about the putty? The putty has properties of both liquids and solids. Like a liquid, it flows when the force is applied slowly. Like a solid, putty snaps when the force is applied quickly.

(*Left*), Pulling slowly on silicon putty
(*Right*), Giving silicon putty a sharp tug

Oceanic crust

Continental crust

LITHOSPHERE
Earth's rigid outer layer is the lithosphere. It includes the crust and solid upper part of the mantle.

ASTHENOSPHERE
The layer just below the lithosphere, in the upper mantle, is the asthenosphere. It is made up of rock that is hot, soft, and slightly fluid.

▲ Layers of Earth's crust and upper mantle

The **asthenosphere** (as then'ə sfir), the layer of Earth below the lithosphere, is not rigid.

The upper part of the asthenosphere is made of rock that behaves like a plastic and is much like silicon putty when the putty is gently stretched. The rock in the lower asthenosphere is partially melted.

Convection currents in a pot of boiling pasta ▼

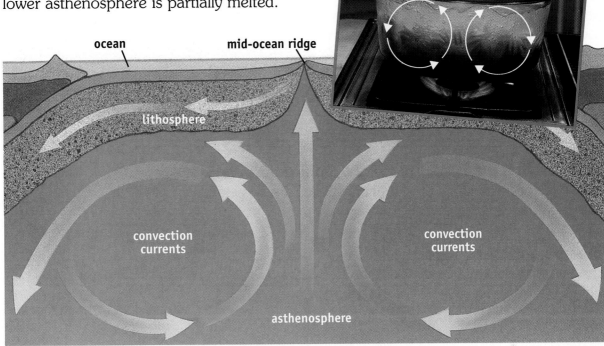

ocean   mid-ocean ridge

lithosphere

convection currents

convection currents

asthenosphere

▲ Convection currents in the asthenosphere are thought to drive the movement of the tectonic plates.

Heating and Cooling Rock

Scientists think that Earth's plates move over its surface because of convection in the asthenosphere. **Convection** (kən-vek'shən) is a process by which energy is transferred by a moving fluid. Convection occurs when a fluid is placed between a hot lower surface and a cold upper surface. A **convection current** is the path along which the energy is transferred.

You are probably familiar with several kinds of convection currents. Have you ever watched rice or pasta whirl around in a pot of boiling water? Convection currents are set in motion when water or air is heated. The heated fluid then rises because it is less dense than the surrounding fluid. In a pot of rice or pasta, when the heated water reaches the top of the pot, it cools and flows back down to begin another journey around the pot. When you did the activity on pages B36 and B37, you saw the effect of convection currents as you watched the movement of the hot and cold water in the aquarium.

Convection in the Mantle

How does convection occur in Earth's mantle? The partly melted hot rock in the asthenosphere rises because it is less dense than the surrounding materials. It slowly makes its way toward the lithosphere. When the melted rock reaches the cooler lithosphere, the melted rock begins to cool and harden. The cooler rock then moves horizontally along the bottom of the lithosphere. When the rock reaches the edge of a plate, it sinks down under the plate into the mantle. As the rock moves down into the asthenosphere, it begins to melt, and the cycle starts again.

Moving Tectonic Plates

Today scientists generally agree that convection currents in the asthenosphere are the force that moves tectonic plates. Recall from Chapter 1 that Alfred Wegener, despite all his evidence, could not explain what caused the continents to move over Earth's surface. Thus, his idea of continental drift was a hypothesis, or a guess based on observations. In the 1960s the theory of plate tectonics was

HOW PLATES INTERACT

Places where plates interact are called **plate boundaries**. Examples of three kinds of interacting plates are shown on this page and the next.

COLLIDING PLATES Plates collide, or come together, at **convergent boundaries**. What do you think might happen when two enormous slabs of rock collide? What kinds of features do you think you'll find along convergent boundaries?

▲ Colliding plates

SEPARATING PLATES Plates move away from one another at **divergent boundaries**. Most divergent boundaries are found on the ocean floor. These boundaries are places where new oceanic crust forms through the process of sea-floor spreading. The photograph shows a divergent boundary.

▲ The walls of this riverbank in Iceland are on plates that separated.

proposed. A theory carries more weight than a hypothesis because a theory is an idea that is supported by evidence. And a theory can be used to make accurate predictions about future events. The **theory of plate tectonics** states that Earth's crust and upper mantle are made up of a series of rigid or nearly rigid plates that are in motion. The map on this page shows these plates and the direction in which they move. ■

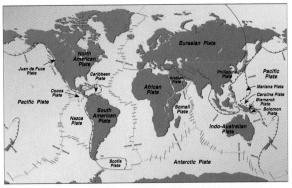

▲ This map shows the location of Earth's major tectonic plates. A full-size map is on pages B20 and B21.

SLIDING PLATES Plates move past one another at **transform-fault boundaries**. A fault is a very large crack in Earth's rocks, along which movement has taken place. The photograph shows the San Andreas Fault, found in the western United States. This fault, one of the longest and most famous in the world, is the site of many earthquakes.

▲ San Andreas Fault, California, as seen from an airplane

INVESTIGATION 1

1. Can convergent and divergent plate boundaries be considered opposites? Write a paragraph comparing these two kinds of plate boundaries.

2. Define the term *tectonic plate* and explain what might cause tectonic plates to move.

THINK IT WRITE IT

HOW DOES THE MOTION OF TECTONIC PLATES BUILD MOUNTAINS?

The tectonic plates that make up Earth's surface are large, thick, and massive. When they move, something has to give! Find out what "gives" in Investigation 2.

Activity

Colliding Plates

MATERIALS
- sheet of cardboard
- tectonic-plates map
- Earth-features map
- *Science Notebook*

Plates are enormously big and heavy. What might happen when one plate runs into another? In this activity you'll demonstrate a simple model of colliding plates.

- -

Procedure

1. Imagine that the sheet of cardboard is a tectonic plate and that a wall is another tectonic plate. Predict what will happen when the two plates collide. Record your predictions.

2. Take the sheet of cardboard and press one edge of it firmly against a wall and push.

3. In your *Science Notebook,* record what happens to the cardboard.

4. Your map of the tectonic plates shows the edges of tectonic plates and the directions in which the plates are moving. Study your map and find one or more places where the boundary between plates is a convergent boundary.

Step 1

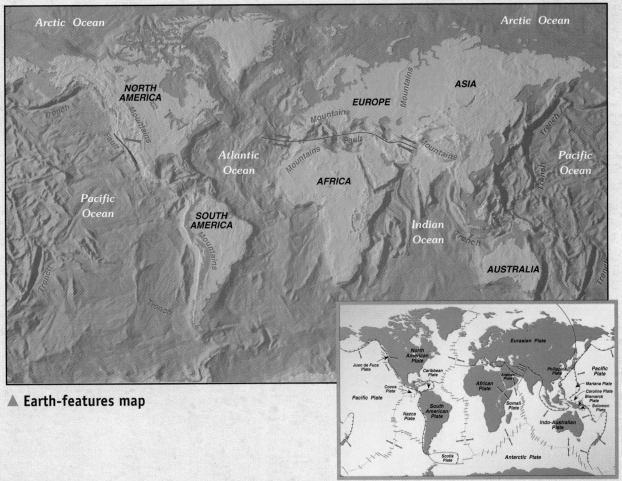

▲ Earth-features map

▲ Tectonic-plates map. For the full-size map, see pages B20 and B21.

5. Form a hypothesis about what happens when two plates meet at a convergent boundary.

Analyze and Conclude

1. What feature forms when two plates collide at a convergent boundary? Locate several such features on the Earth-features map.

2. In what parts of the world are two plates now colliding? Infer how these regions may change in the future.

UNIT PROJECT LINK

After several earthquakes shook California in the 1990s, the Sierra Nevada range became more than 0.3 m (1 ft) taller. What other mountains in the world are still growing? Use newspapers and magazines to find out about earthquakes and volcanoes that have recently lifted mountains. Find out what form of mountain building caused the uplift. Use a map to identify the location of the growing mountains.

B43

Activity
A Big Fender Bender

MATERIALS
- 2 cellulose sponges
- water
- *Science Notebook*

Think about what happens when two cars collide. What happens to the metal? What do you think happens when two continents collide? You'll use a simple model to find out.

Procedure

1. Form a hypothesis about what you think will happen when one continent bumps into another. Discuss your hypothesis with other members of your group. Record your hypothesis in your *Science Notebook*.

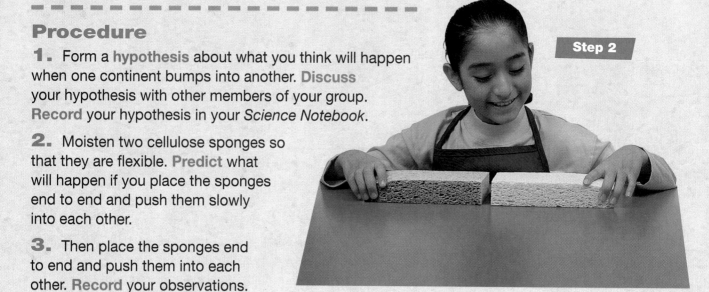

Step 2

2. Moisten two cellulose sponges so that they are flexible. Predict what will happen if you place the sponges end to end and push them slowly into each other.

3. Then place the sponges end to end and push them into each other. Record your observations.

Analyze and Conclude

1. What did you observe?

2. Did the sponges do what you predicted they would do? If not, what was different?

3. Explain how the moist sponges are a model of continents colliding. How is this model related to what you did in the preceding activity?

INVESTIGATE FURTHER!

RESEARCH

When North America collided with North Africa to form part of Pangaea, a large mountain range was thrust upward on the North American Plate. Find out which mountains they were and what has happened to them.

B44

Mountain-Building

Have you ever gone mountain climbing? A mountain is any feature that rises above the surrounding landscape. So whether you've climbed the steep slopes of the Rocky Mountains or just hiked a local hill, you've gone mountain climbing!

Mountains form as the result of four basic processes: folding, faulting, doming, and volcanic activity—so mountains can be classified as folded mountains, fault-block mountains, dome mountains, or volcanoes. Three of these kinds of mountains—folded, fault-block, and volcanic—result from plate movements.

Folded Mountains

Have you ever made a paper fan? If you have, then you've squeezed paper to make a series of pleats, or folds. If you were to look at the folded edge of the fan, you would see a series of crests, or high points, and troughs, or low points. Folded mountains form when masses of rock are squeezed from opposite sides. In the activities on pages B42 to B44, you saw that folded mountains form when two plates collide. The Appalachians, the Alps, the Urals, and the Himalayas can be classified as folded mountains. Locate these mountain ranges on a globe of Earth.

FOLDED MOUNTAINS These form when two tectonic plates collide.

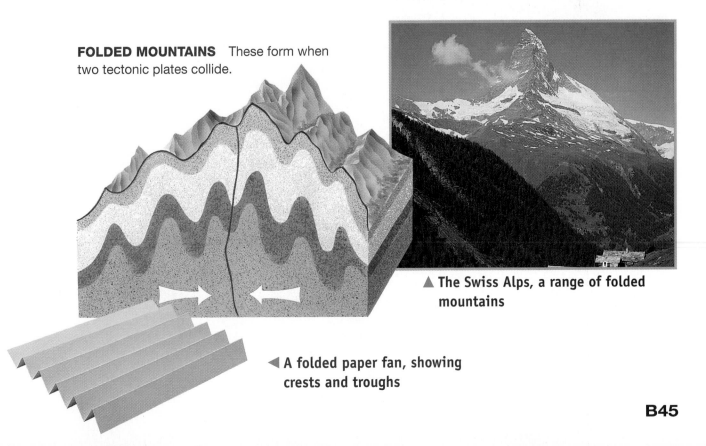

▲ **The Swiss Alps, a range of folded mountains**

◄ **A folded paper fan, showing crests and troughs**

Fault-block Mountains

Recall that a fault is a large crack in Earth's rocks, along which movement has taken place. Forces produced by moving plates can move rock along faults. When blocks of rock move up or down along a fault, a mountain can form.

Examples of fault-block mountains include those in the Dead Sea area, the Grand Tetons in Wyoming, and those in the Great Rift Valley of Africa. Among the mountains in the Great Rift Valley, scientists have unearthed some of the oldest known human fossils.

Dome Mountains

Have you ever heard of Pikes Peak? This granite summit in the Colorado Rockies is 4,341 m (14,110 ft) tall! It was explored in 1806 by Zebulon Pike. Although the peak was eventually named after him, Pike never even reached its summit! Pikes Peak is a dome mountain that formed millions of years ago when forces deep within Earth pushed magma toward the surface, where it cooled and hardened. Although dome mountains have an igneous core, sedimentary rocks can border such mountains. But erosion often strips away the sedimentary rocks to reveal the harder igneous core.

Other dome mountains in the United States are the Sangre de Cristo Mountains, the Bighorn Mountains, the Black Hills, and Longs Peak. Find these dome mountains on a map of the United States. Are any of them in your state or in nearby states?

SCIENCE IN LITERATURE

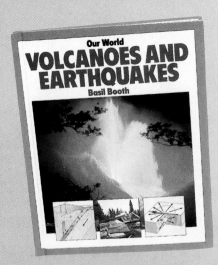

VOLCANOES AND EARTHQUAKES
by Basil Booth
Silver Burdett Press, 1991

Reference books are good sources when you want to find information about a specific topic.

Read pages 18–19 in *Volcanoes and Earthquakes* to find out how the Andes Mountain range of South America and the Cascade Range of North America were formed. Then try to explain to a classmate how water trapped in crustal rocks is related to mountain building. When you get to Chapters 3 and 4 in this unit, use *Volcanoes and Earthquakes* to find the answers to your own questions.

FAULT-BLOCK MOUNTAINS These mountains form when masses of rock move up or down along a fault.

▲ Wasatch Range, Utah, fault-block mountains

DOME MOUNTAINS These mountains form when the surface is lifted up by magma, forming a broad dome, or bulge. Wind and rain erode the dome, stripping away layers of sedimentary rock and exposing the igneous rock below.

▲ Pikes Peak, Colorado, a dome mountain

INVESTIGATE FURTHER!

EXPERIMENT

Use a few different colors of modeling clay to demonstrate how folded mountains form. Then use the clay and a plastic knife to show how fault-block mountains form. USE CARE IN HANDLING THE KNIFE. Make sketches of your models in your *Science Notebook*.

Volcanoes

Have you ever opened a bottle of warm soda and had it spray all over you? The spraying of the soda is a bit like the eruption of magma when a volcano forms. **Volcanoes**, a fourth type of mountain, are common along convergent and divergent plate boundaries. They form when magma, or molten rock, erupts from an opening in Earth's surface. Sometimes the eruption is quiet; at other times it is quite forceful.

Mount St. Helens is a volcano in the Cascade Range. This mountain chain extends from northern California to British Columbia, in Canada. On May 18, 1980, Mount St. Helens blew its top and threw dust, ash, and volcanic rocks 18,000 m (59,400 ft) above the ground! As the ash rained back down to Earth, it blanketed some places with as much as 2 m (6.6 ft) of fine material. In some places the ash was so thick that it looked like midnight when it was actually noon! You will learn much more about volcanoes in Chapter 4. ■

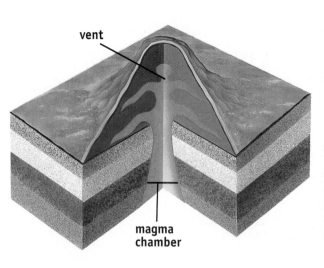

▲ A typical volcano

Mount St. Helens, Washington State. (*Top*), before the 1980 eruption; (*middle*), during the eruption; and (*bottom*), after the eruption.

Life at the Top

You now know that folded mountains are formed by the interactions of tectonic plates. The Himalaya Mountains, for example, were formed millions of years ago when the plate carrying India, then a separate continent, rammed into the plate carrying Asia. This enormous collision of plates crumpled the crust and lifted up sediment from the ocean floor, forming the Himalayas. In some places the sediment was raised up thousands of meters, forming folded mountains.

People used to living at low altitudes experience problems as they move up into higher country. Climbers of very high mountains—the Himalayas, for example—can experience many difficulties. Newcomers experience problems with breathing. The lower air pressure at higher altitudes means that less oxygen is taken in with each breath. A lack of oxygen can affect vision and make walking dangerous. Heart rate quickens sharply, and the heart tries to supply more oxygen to the body. Climbers often have to stop to rest every few meters.

People in Nepal, a country in the Himalayas, have adapted to living high

The world's highest mountains, compared to the Empire State Building ▼

9000 m

Mt. Everest
ASIA
8,708.4 m

Mt. Aconcagua
SOUTH AMERICA
6,850.2 m

Mt. McKinley
NORTH AMERICA
6,096 m

Mt. Kilimanjaro
AFRICA
5,802 m

Mt. Elbrus
EUROPE
5,633 m

Mt. Vinson Massif
ANTARCTICA
5,058.9 m

Empire State Building
NORTH AMERICA
448.6 m

0 m

▲ Tenzing Norgay climbed Mount Everest.

▲ Sherpa women in their mountain village

up in the mountains. Nepal is the home of the highest mountain peak in the world—Mount Everest, which towers 8,848 m (29,028 ft) above sea level.

The Sherpas, a people of Tibetan ancestry who live mainly in Nepal, are known for their ability to live and work in the high terrain of their country. How have the Sherpas adapted to their life high in the mountains?

The Sherpas' most important adaptation has to do with their blood. Because the Sherpas have lived all their lives in the mountains, their blood contains more oxygen-carrying red blood cells than that of most other people. So, with each breath the Sherpas take, they can absorb more available oxygen and pump it throughout their bodies. The ability to move enough oxygen throughout the body prevents many problems. In fact, Tenzing Norgay, a Sherpa, was one of the first two men to climb to the top of Mount Everest!

Visitors to the high mountains adapt to the lower air pressure after several weeks. What happens? Like the bodies of the native peoples, their bodies produce more of the oxygen-carrying red blood cells. In time, newcomers to the high mountains can also pump more oxygen throughout their bodies. ■

INVESTIGATION 2

1. How are folded mountains like fault-block mountains? How are the two kinds of mountains different? Write a paragraph comparing and contrasting these kinds of mountains.

2. Describe the relationship between the collision of plates and the formation of mountains.

REFLECT & EVALUATE

WORD POWER

asthenosphere   convection
plate boundary   volcano
dome mountain   lithosphere
convection current
convergent boundary
divergent boundary
fault-block mountain
folded mountain
theory of plate tectonics
transform-fault boundary

 On Your Own
Define each term.

With a Partner
Scramble the letters of each term in the list. With terms of two or more words, keep the scrambled letters separate for each word. Exchange scrambled terms with your partner. Who can unscramble them first?

PORTFOLIO

Collect photos of mountains. Classify them as folded, fault-block, dome, or volcano. Make a poster of your collection.

Analyze Information

The map below shows a convergent boundary between two tectonic plates. Describe what features you might see along this convergent boundary.

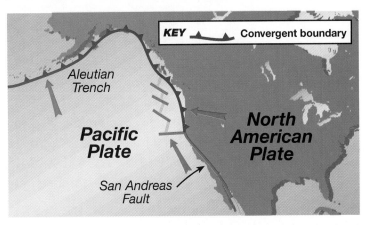

Assess Performance

Make a double-decker peanut-butter-and-jelly sandwich. Cut it in half and use it to show how fault-block mountains are formed.

Problem Solving

1. Imagine that you are in a special kind of submarine that has entered Earth's upper mantle. The submarine is riding along in the convection currents. Describe your journey.

2. You skid on a small rug into a wall. How is what happens to the rug like tectonic plates building mountains?

3. The San Andreas Fault in California is a transform-fault boundary between the North American Plate and the Pacific Plate. Describe and model how the plates are moving along this boundary.

CHAPTER 3

SHAKE, RATTLE, AND ROLL

Many men and women in science try to solve problems that affect people's daily lives. Earthquakes have terrified people throughout history, and they continue to threaten loss of life and property today. How can science help?

Scientists on the Scene

Among the first people to investigate an earthquake are the seismologists (sīz mäl' ə jists). These scientists study how and why earthquakes happen. Waverly Person is the chief of the National Earthquake Information Service in Denver, Colorado. He and his staff monitor movements in Earth's crust, using seismographs and other technology.

Seismologists examine the strength of each earthquake, how long it lasts, and where it is located. They exchange ideas about *why* an earthquake has happened. Over the years, seismologists have developed hypotheses about where future earthquakes will happen. How might such predictions be useful?

Coming Up

◄ Waverly Person checking a seismograph

WHAT CAUSES EARTH-QUAKES AND HOW CAN THEY BE COMPARED?

Picture two railroad cars rolling by each other on side-by-side tracks. Could they get past each other if their sides were touching? Some tectonic plates are a little like these trains. This investigation is about the sudden changes that can occur when plates that touch move past one another.

Activity

A Model of Sliding Plates

Did you ever try to slide a heavy box over a rough sidewalk and have the box get stuck? Tectonic plates have rough surfaces, too. What happens when the plates keep pushing but the rocks don't slide?

Procedure

1. Cover two blocks of wood with coarse sandpaper. Use rubber bands, as shown, to hold the sandpaper on the blocks of wood.

2. **Predict** what will happen if you hold the sandpaper surfaces tightly against each other and then try to slide the blocks past each other. **Record** your prediction in your *Science Notebook*.

Step 1

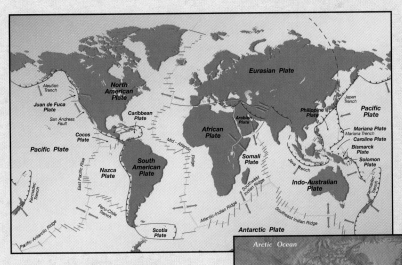

▲ Tectonic-plates map. For a larger map, see pages B20 and B21.

3. Try sliding the blocks past each other. (Hold together the surfaces on which there are no rubber bands.) **Observe** what happens and **record** your observations.

4. Explain how this action might be like two tectonic plates passing each other.

5. Now list the places shown on your tectonic-plates map where plates are sliding past each other. For example, note that the Pacific Plate and the North American Plate are sliding past each other near the west coast of the United States.

6. Find the same places on the Earth-features map. List any features you find in those places that seem to be related to the motion of the plates.

Analyze and Conclude

1. Think about the places you identified in steps 5 and 6. Have you read or heard anything about either of these locations that might involve changes in Earth's crust? What do you conclude might happen when two tectonic plates slide past each other?

2. Did you find anything that looks like it might be caused by the sliding of two plates? If so, what did you find?

▲ Earth-features map. For a larger map, see page B43.

INVESTIGATE FURTHER!

EXPERIMENT

Find two bricks. Slide one over the other. Do they slide easily? What do you hear? What do you feel? What happens when two smooth rock surfaces slide past each other?

Sliding Plates

OVER 500 DEAD, $200,000,000 LOST IN SAN FRANCISCO EARTHQUAKE

Nearly Half the City Is in Ruins and 50,000 Are Homeless.

VOL. LV...NO. 17,617.   • • • • •   NEW YORK, THUR

firemen and United States soldiers, who assisted them, blew down building after building. Their efforts, however, were useless, so far as checking the headway of the flames was concerned. The shortage of water was due to the breaking of the mains of the Spring Valley Water Company at San Mateo. The water needed so badly in the city raid in a flood over San Mateo.

Burning of the Opera House.

▲ City Hall after the 1906 San Francisco earthquake; a 1906 newspaper headline

It was a little after 5:00 A.M. on April 18, 1906. Many San Franciscans were awakened by a deep rumbling of the ground beneath them. Homes, stores, offices, hotels, churches, and bridges collapsed. Sergeant Jesse Cook, a police officer, observed, "The whole street was undulating [waving]. It was as if the waves of the ocean were coming toward me."

An editor from the *Examiner* newspaper noted that trolley tracks were twisted like wriggling snakes and that water and gas spurted high into the air.

Scientists estimate that the earthquake that struck San Francisco in 1906 would have had a reading of about 8.3 on the Richter scale. (You'll read more about the Richter scale in "Our Active Earth" on pages B58 and B59.) The earthquake

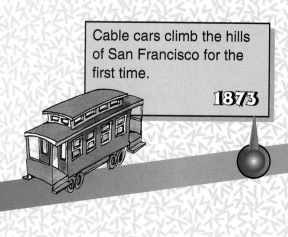

Cable cars climb the hills of San Francisco for the first time.

1873

Gold is discovered at Sutter's Mill.

1848

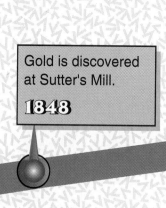

lasted for only a little over a minute. But its effects were enormous. About 500 people died, and nearly 250,000 were left homeless. Water mains were destroyed. Fires due to broken gas lines raged throughout the city for days. More than 28,000 buildings were destroyed by the fires.

Shortly after the quake, San Franciscans began to rebuild their destroyed city and their disrupted lives. By December 1906, many new buildings stood where others had collapsed. Within about three years, 20,000 buildings had been constructed to replace those lost to fire and to the quake itself.

Today, just as in 1906, people ask "What are earthquakes? Why do these tremors happen in some places and not in others?" An earthquake is a vibration of the Earth, caused by a sudden release of energy stored in the crust. Most earthquakes occur along tectonic plate boundaries, places on Earth where vast slabs of rock separate, collide, or slide past one another.

Faults

The 1906 earthquake occurred when blocks of rock deep within Earth's surface began to move along a crack called the San Andreas Fault. A fault is a large crack in layers of rock along which movement has occurred. The San Andreas Fault runs through much of California and separates the North American Plate from the Pacific Plate. The 1906 San Francisco earthquake wasn't the first "earth-shaking" event to occur along the San Andreas Fault and it wasn't the last. Many large earthquakes have struck that region since 1906. A major earthquake struck the San Francisco Bay area in October 1989. That quake, measuring 7.1 on the Richter scale, caused $7 billion in damage and 63 deaths. Scientists predict that a much larger earthquake—the "Big One"—is yet to come. ■

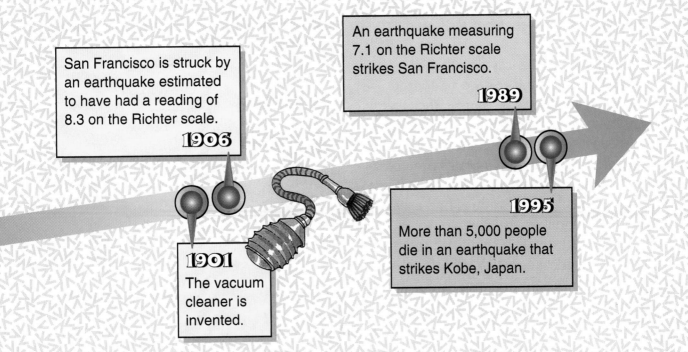

San Francisco is struck by an earthquake estimated to have had a reading of 8.3 on the Richter scale.
1906

An earthquake measuring 7.1 on the Richter scale strikes San Francisco.
1989

1901
The vacuum cleaner is invented.

1995
More than 5,000 people die in an earthquake that strikes Kobe, Japan.

Our Active Earth

Earth is an ever-changing planet. Some changes happen in a matter of seconds or minutes. Other changes occur over months or years. Soils are eroded by water, wind, and gravity. Mountains take hundreds, thousands, or even millions of years to form and just as long to be worn away. And some changes, such as those caused by earthquakes, occur suddenly and violently.

Earthquakes

Earthquakes usually last for only a few minutes. But it takes many years to build up the energy that is released during an earthquake. As blocks of rocks move past one another along faults, friction prevents some sections of rock from slipping very much. Instead, the rocks bend and change shape, until the force becomes too great. It is only when the rocks suddenly slide past each other that an earthquake occurs.

An **earthquake** is a vibration of Earth, caused by the release of energy that has been stored in Earth's rocks as they have ground past one another over time. Most earthquakes occur in parts of the world where tectonic plates are colliding, separating, or moving horizontally past each other. California is one area where earthquakes are likely to occur. Part of southern California is on the edge of the Pacific Plate, which is moving slowly toward the northwest.

The San Andreas Fault

During the 30-million-year history of the San Andreas Fault in California, hundreds of earthquakes and many thousands of aftershocks have occurred along its length of 1,200 km (720 mi). An **aftershock** is a shock that occurs after the principal shock of an earthquake. Recall that one of these tremors nearly destroyed the city of San Francisco in 1906.

A more recent earthquake, which was centered in Loma Prieta, California, in October 1989, was felt as far away as Oregon and Nevada. This earthquake caused more than 60 deaths and registered 7.1 on the Richter scale.

Damage caused by the Loma Prieta, California, earthquake in October 1989. ▼

The Richter Scale

If you've ever listened to or read a news report about an earthquake, you've heard the term *Richter scale*. The **Richter scale**, with numbers ranging from 1 to 10, describes the magnitude, or strength, of an earthquake. The **magnitude** of an earthquake is the amount of energy released by the quake. The Richter scale is named after the American seismologist Charles Richter.

Minor earthquakes have magnitudes of 4 or less. The largest recorded earthquakes have magnitudes of about 8.5.

Each increase of 1.0 on the Richter scale represents a difference of about 30 times more energy than the previous number. For example, an earthquake measuring 5.0 on the Richter scale releases about 30 times more energy than a quake measuring 4.0. Likewise, an earthquake measuring 5.7 on the

The Pacific Plate and North American Plate border the San Andreas Fault. In which directions do the plates move? ▼

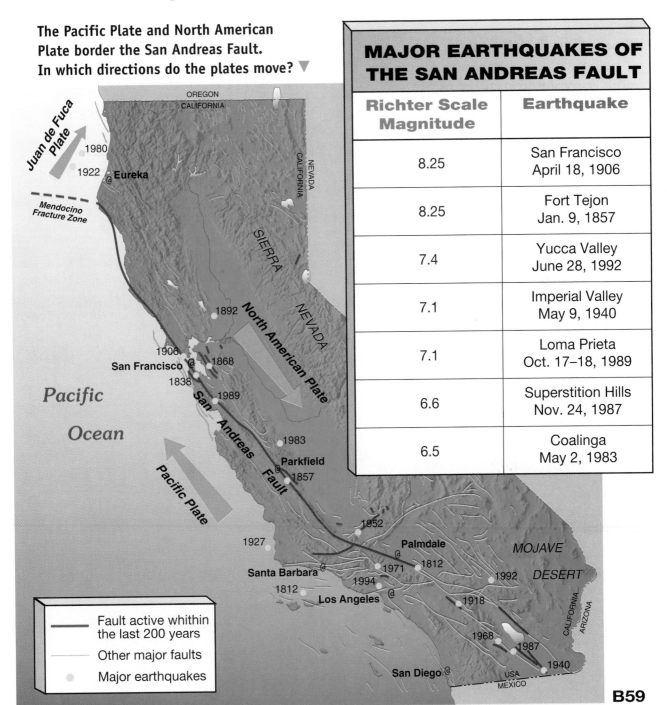

MAJOR EARTHQUAKES OF THE SAN ANDREAS FAULT	
Richter Scale Magnitude	**Earthquake**
8.25	San Francisco April 18, 1906
8.25	Fort Tejon Jan. 9, 1857
7.4	Yucca Valley June 28, 1992
7.1	Imperial Valley May 9, 1940
7.1	Loma Prieta Oct. 17–18, 1989
6.6	Superstition Hills Nov. 24, 1987
6.5	Coalinga May 2, 1983

Legend:
— Fault active whithin the last 200 years
— Other major faults
● Major earthquakes

Richter scale releases about 30 times less energy than an earthquake measuring 6.7 on the scale.

Now study the table and map on page B59, showing some of the earthquakes that occurred along the San Andreas Fault over the past century. Where along the San Andreas did most of the quakes occur? Where did the strongest earthquakes occur? Then look at the map below. Where is the strongest quake likely to occur in the future?

Predicting Earthquakes

Scientists know that earthquakes are more common in some parts of the world than in others. Yet the actual timing of these Earth movements is difficult to predict. Seismologists, scientists who study earthquakes, have no sure way of knowing when or where an earthquake will strike or how strong it will be. They can only give estimates of the probability that an earthquake will strike in a certain place within a certain span of years.

Once in a while, seismologists are lucky in predicting earthquakes. In 1988, seismologists of the United States Geological Survey predicted that Loma Prieta, California, was likely to have an earthquake. Loma Prieta is along the San Andreas Fault. On October 17, 1989, a severe earthquake struck Loma Prieta and nearby San Francisco and Oakland.

Seismologists have found that there are changes in Earth that come before most earthquakes. Knowing this, the seismologists closely watch instruments that measure and record these changes. Seismologists are especially careful to

A map of California showing how likely it is that the "Big One" will strike in different parts of the state ▼

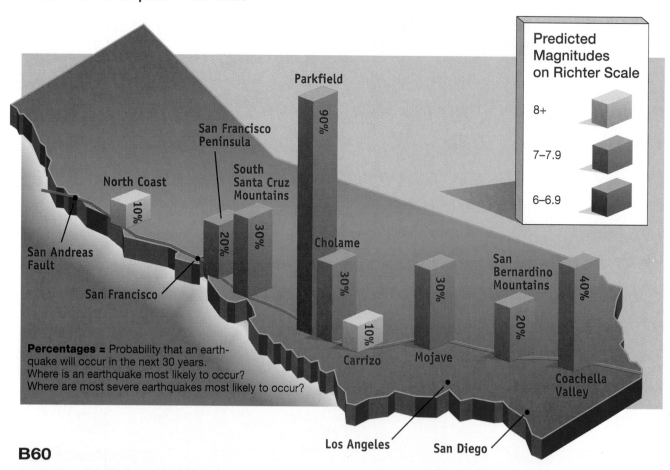

watch the instruments in regions where earthquakes are likely to occur. For example, changes in the tilt of slabs of rock below ground can indicate that an earthquake is brewing. Studies have shown that rock formations will swell before an earthquake. Changes in Earth's magnetic and gravitational fields can mean an earthquake is soon to strike. Increases in the amount of a radioactive gas called radon from within Earth often come before an earthquake. Micro-earthquakes, or minor tremors, can also indicate that a more intense earthquake will strike an area.

Just how accurate are these warnings? Some scientists argue that watching changes in various instruments can lead to the prediction of earthquakes. Eleven days before the 1989 Loma Prieta earthquake, an instrument in the area recorded natural radio waves from Earth that were nearly 30 times stronger than usual. Just a few hours before the earthquake struck, these radio signals became so strong that they shot off the scale of the instrument.

A study by scientists at the Southern California Earthquake Center suggests that in the next 30 years there will be a severe earthquake in southern California. Exactly when and where it will strike is anyone's guess. ■

▲ **Laser beams are being used to monitor Earth's movements and to predict quakes.**

INVESTIGATE FURTHER!

....

RESEARCH

Some people believe that animals are very sensitive to the changes that occur before events such as storms and earthquakes. Find out about this hypothesis concerning animal behavior before an earthquake as a possible warning sign for people. What do you think about this idea?

═══════════════ **INVESTIGATION 1** ═══════════════

1. You are writing a news report on an earthquake that has just occurred. Tell your readers where and why the quake occurred, which plates were involved, and how severe it was.

2. Explain how the movement of tectonic plates and the occurrence of earthquakes are related.

WHAT HAPPENS TO EARTH'S CRUST DURING AN EARTHQUAKE?

Have you ever pushed a desk across a floor? Sometimes the desk starts to vibrate, and you can feel the vibrations in your hands and arms. In this investigation you'll find out how this experience is similar to what happens during an earthquake.

Activity
Shake It!

In this activity you'll make a model for observing what can happen to buildings during an earthquake. In your model you'll make the vibrations.

MATERIALS
- small block of wood
- clear plastic bowl, filled with sand
- water
- measuring cup
- clear plastic bowl, filled with gelatin
- *Science Notebook*

Procedure

1. Think of a block of wood as a building and a bowl filled with sand as the surface of Earth. Stand a block of wood in a bowl full of sand.

2. **Predict** what will happen if you shake the bowl. **Record** your predictions in your *Science Notebook*.

A highway toppled during the 1995 earthquake in Kobe, Japan. ▶

3. Shake the bowl rapidly by sliding it back and forth. Observe what happens to the block and the surface of the sand. Record your observations.

4. Pour water over the sand until the water is at the same level as the sand. Again stand the wooden block on the sand. Predict what will happen to the block if you shake the bowl with the wet sand. Repeat the shaking, observe what happens, and record your observations.

5. Now predict what will happen when you set the block on the gelatin and shake the bowl. Try it; then record your observations.

Analyze and Conclude

1. During the "earthquake," what happened to the dry sand? the wet sand? the gelatin? What, do you think, did the dry sand, wet sand, and the gelatin represent?

2. What happened to the "building" as it stood on the different surfaces?

3. Which model showed the most damage to the "building"? What evidence supports your conclusions?

UNIT PROJECT LINK

At 5:30 P.M. on March 27, 1964, the most powerful earthquake to hit North America struck Anchorage, Alaska. More than 130 people in Alaska and 12 people in Crescent City, California, were killed by the tsunami that followed the quake. (You'll find out about tsunamis on pages B76–77.) Use a map to trace how far the tsunami traveled. Then compute the distance that the tsunami traveled. Look at an earthquake map of the world. Outline in red those North American coastlines that might experience tsunamis.

Bend
Till It Breaks

Imagine that you are holding a flexible wooden stick that is about 2 cm wide and 1 m long. You are holding one end in each hand and are gently bending the stick. If you stop bending the stick, it will return to its original shape. What will happen if you keep on bending it? Eventually it will snap!

Forces and Faults

Although Earth's rocks are hard and brittle, in some ways they can behave like the bending wooden stick. You probably know that a force is a push or a pull. If a pulling force is applied slowly to rocks, they will stretch. But like the wooden stick, the rocks will break or snap if the

Movement Along Faults

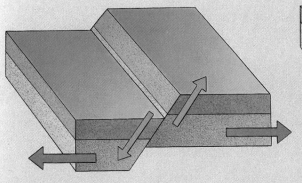

NORMAL FAULT The rock slabs are pulling apart, and one slab has moved up, while the other has moved down along the fault.

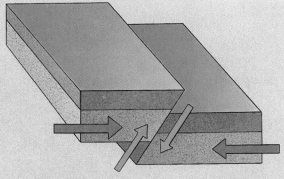

REVERSE FAULT The rock slabs are pushing together, and one rock slab has pushed under the other along the fault.

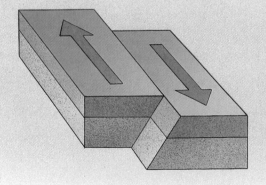

STRIKE-SLIP FAULT Slabs of rock are moving horizontally past each other along a fault. This type of fault is produced by twisting and tearing of layers of rock. The San Andreas Fault is an example of a strike-slip fault.

force on them is too great. A break in rocks along which the rocks have moved is called a **fault**.

What do you think would happen if rocks are squeezed together from opposite sides? If pushing forces are applied to rocks, they bend, or fold. But, just as with pulling forces, pushing forces will eventually cause rocks to break. So, pushing forces also create faults in rocks. You can see the effect of these pushing forces in the drawing of the reverse fault on page B64.

Movement Along Faults

Forces may continue to be applied to slabs of rock that contain faults. The forces, which may be either up-and-down or sideways, may continue for many years. The three drawings on page B64 show examples of the main kinds of movement along faults. In time, the forces on the rocks become so great that the slabs overcome the friction that has held them together. Then the rock slabs move violently along the fault.

Earthquakes and Faults

Imagine that your two hands are the two rock walls on either side of a fault. Picture rubbing your hands together when they are in soapy water. Then picture rubbing them together when they are dry. Sometimes the movement of rocks along a fault is quick and smooth, like the rubbing together of soap-covered hands. But at other times, as with dry hands rubbed together, the movement can be slow and rough. As the movement causes rocks to lock and bend, energy builds up in the rocks, much as energy builds up in a flexed wooden stick. When the energy in the rocks is released, an earthquake occurs.

You know that an earthquake is a vibration of the Earth produced by the quick release of this stored energy. The point at which an earthquake begins is the **focus** of the earthquake. Most earthquakes begin below the surface. The point on Earth's surface directly above the focus is called the **epicenter** (ep′ə sen tər) of the earthquake.

Earthquakes can begin anywhere from about 5 km (about 3 mi) to 700 km (about 430 mi) below Earth's surface. Scientists have found that most earthquakes are shallow—they occur within 60 km (about 35 mi) of the surface. The most destructive earthquakes seem to be the shallow ones. The focus of the 1906 San Francisco earthquake was no deeper than about 15 km (about 9 mi).

Earthquake Focus and Epicenter

Waves are sent out in all directions from the focus of the earthquake. Notice that the epicenter is the spot on the surface of Earth that lies directly above the focus. ▼

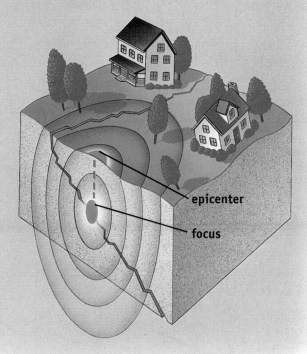

epicenter

focus

Earthquakes Around the World

When earthquake locations are plotted on a world map, patterns emerge. From the map on page B17 you can see that earthquakes occur along certain belts, or zones. Do these zones look familiar? They should! Most earthquakes occur along tectonic plate boundaries. Many occur near the edges of the Pacific Ocean.

Japan, the western United States, Chile, and parts of Central America are just a few of the areas around the edges of the Pacific Ocean that experience earthquakes.

Where do most earthquakes occur in the United States? Even without looking at a map, you probably could have guessed that most earthquakes in the United States happen in California. Now look closely at the map on page B17. Some earthquakes have occurred in the eastern part of the country—far away from the San Andreas Fault. Is your area at risk for an earthquake? Although most earthquakes occur in California, earthquakes are possible anywhere in this country. What is the risk that your state or surrounding states will experience an earthquake?

Earthquake Waves

Have you ever stood in a pool, lake, or ocean and felt water waves break against your body? Have you ever "done the wave" at a sporting event? What do all waves have in common? A wave is a

SCIENCE IN LITERATURE

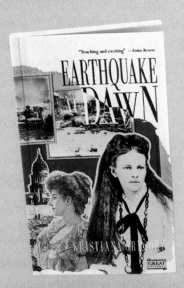

EARTHQUAKE AT DAWN
by Kristiana Gregory
Harcourt Brace, 1992

It was an April morning in 1906. Aboard a boat in San Francisco harbor, 15-year-old Daisy Valentine thought the boat had struck a rock. Then there was an explosive booming sound. The city of San Francisco went dark. Someone on board screamed "Earthquake!"

Daisy Valentine, who tells the story *Earthquake at Dawn*, is a fictional character. But another character, Edith Irvine, really did take that boat ride to San Francisco. Edith, a young photographer, spent the next few days among the fires, ruins, and tragedy resulting from this famous earthquake. In *Earthquake at Dawn* you'll find Edith's photographs of the devastation and read a letter from an eyewitness.

rhythmic disturbance that carries energy. The energy released by an earthquake travels in all directions from the earthquake's focus. There are three kinds of earthquake waves: P waves, S waves, and L waves. The drawings below show how these waves differ. ■

Earthquakes can severely damage property. ▶

P WAVES   P waves move out in all directions from the earthquake focus. The primary waves push and pull the rocks causing them to vibrate in the same direction in which the wave is traveling.

S WAVES   S waves move out in all directions from the earthquake focus. The secondary waves cause the rocks to move at right angles to the direction in which the wave is traveling.

L WAVES   When the P and S waves punch into Earth's surface, they cause the formation of L waves or surface waves. L waves move along the surface causing rocks to move up and down. These are the most destructive earthquake waves.

INVESTIGATION 2

1. Describe and make drawings of the changes taking place in Earth's crust during an earthquake. Explain the forces that caused these changes.

2. What is the connection between a fault and the production of an earthquake? Give a well-known example of such a connection.

HOW ARE EARTHQUAKES LOCATED AND MEASURED?

The newscaster read, "The earthquake last night in Prince William Sound, Alaska, measured 8.4 on the Richter scale. It was a BIG one!" What tools and methods do scientists use to measure how strong an earthquake is or where it began?

Activity

Shake It Harder!

The energy of an earthquake is measured with a device called a seismograph. In this activity you'll build a working model of a seismograph and then test how it works as you create your own small "earthquake."

MATERIALS

- string
- chair
- metric ruler
- 2 heavy books
- masking tape
- fine-point marker
- table
- shelf paper (2 m long)
- *Science Notebook*

SAFETY

Be careful not to push or shake the chair off the tabletop while doing this activity.

Procedure

1. Tightly wrap several lengths of string around the seat of a chair in two places (about 10 cm apart), as shown on page B69.

2. Tightly wrap string around two heavy books in two places (about 6 cm from each end of the books).

3. Tape a fine-point marker to one of the short edges of the books. The tip of the marker should hang about 3–4 cm below the edges of the books.

4. Place a length of shelf paper on the top of a table. Place the chair with the string wrapped around the seat on the table, above the shelf paper. Make sure the legs of the chair don't touch the shelf paper.

5. Using string, suspend the books from the chair so that the tip of the marker just touches the surface of the shelf paper. Make sure that the books are parallel to the paper.

Steps 1–4

6. You have just built a simple seismograph. You'll use it to measure an "earthquake" that you'll create by gently shaking the table from side to side. The shelf paper will become the seismogram, or record of the earthquake.

7. Predict what will be shown on the seismogram if you shake the table gently. **Record** your predictions in your *Science Notebook*.

8. Place your hands against the side of the table and gently shake it as another member of your group slowly pulls the paper under the pen.

9. Repeat step 8. This time, shake the table a little harder (move the table farther but not faster).

Analyze and Conclude

1. How did your prediction in step 7 compare with what actually happened?

2. How did changing the energy with which you shook the table change the seismogram? How did the record on the seismogram for the first "earthquake" differ from that for the second "earthquake"?

3. How do you think a real seismograph is like the one you built? How might it be different?

INVESTIGATE FURTHER!

EXPERIMENT

Does the seismograph work as well if you shake the table in the same direction in which the paper is being pulled? What would this mean with a real seismograph? Is there any connection between the length of the strings and the working of the seismograph?

Activity

Locating Earthquakes

The point on Earth's surface directly above the origin of an earthquake is called the epicenter. The location of the epicenter can be found by comparing the travel times of two kinds of energy waves (called P waves and S waves) at different locations.

MATERIALS

- metric ruler
- Earthquake Travel Time graph
- map of the United States
- drawing compass
- *Science Notebook*

Data

The table below shows the times (in Pacific Daylight Saving Time) at which shock waves reached three cities in the United States after the earthquake in California on October 17–18, 1989. You'll use this information to find the exact location of the epicenter of that earthquake.

Procedure

1. In your *Science Notebook*, set up a table like the one shown. For each city, calculate the difference in arrival time between the P wave and the S wave. Record your results.

	ARRIVAL TIMES OF P WAVES AND S WAVES		
City	P Wave Arrival Time (hr: min: sec)	S Wave Arrival Time (hr: min: sec)	Difference in Arrival Time (hr: min: sec)
Tucson, AZ	5:06:35	5:08:50	
Billings, MT	5:07:10	5:10:00	
Houston, TX	5:09:10	5:13:35	

2. Place a sheet of paper along the *y*-axis of the Earthquake Travel Time graph provided by your teacher. On the sheet of paper, mark the time interval between the arrival of the P wave and the S wave in Tucson. For example, if the time difference was 4 minutes, you would make a mark next to "0" and a mark next to "4."

3. Keep the edge of the paper parallel to the *y*-axis. Move the paper to the right until the space between the marks matches the space between the S-wave curve and the P-wave curve.

4. The point on the *x*-axis directly below (or along) the edge of the paper is the distance from Tucson to the epicenter of the quake. **Record** this distance.

5. Repeat steps 2 through 4 for Billings and Houston.

6. On a United States map, use a drawing compass to draw a circle around each city in the chart. Use the calculated distance from the quake as the radius of each circle. The point at which the circles intersect is the epicenter of the October 1989 earthquake.

Step 6

Analyze and Conclude

1. What is the distance from each of the cities to the epicenter?

2. Where was the epicenter of the October 1989 earthquake?

3. What is the lowest number of reporting locations necessary to locate an epicenter? Explain your answer.

4. Compare your results with those of other members of your class. Account for any differences you find.

INVESTIGATE FURTHER!

TAKE ACTION

Contact or visit an office of the U.S. Geological Survey for more information about locating earthquakes. You may write to the U.S. Geological Survey at Distribution Branch, Box 25286, Federal Center, Denver, CO 80225.

Activity

Be an Architect

The competition is stiff! You and your teammates will build an "earthquake-proof" building. Then you will create a mini-earthquake and test your building. Will it remain standing? Which team will have the most earthquake-proof building?

MATERIALS

- several small cardboard boxes
- masking tape
- large aluminum pan
- clay
- sand
- soil
- dowels
- timer with a second hand
- *Science Notebook*

Procedure

1. With other members of your team, design a high-rise "building" that will not tip over in an earthquake. The building must be made of cardboard boxes and any other materials, such as clay, sand, soil, and dowels, that your teacher provides for you. You will subject this building to an "earthquake" that you create by shaking your desk or table. Draw your design in your *Science Notebook*.

2. With the rest of your class, design a standard that describes when a building is considered earthquake-proof. Make sure the standard will clearly separate good designs from poor designs following an earthquake.

3. Construct your building on top of your desk or table.

4. Predict how well your building will withstand an earthquake. Discuss your prediction with other members of your group.

Step 1

5. With the rest of your class, determine how long the earthquake will last and how strongly you'll shake the table. Note the length of time the building remains standing during the earthquake. Note whether the building undergoes any kind of damage during the earthquake. Use the standard to determine if your building is earthquake-proof. **Record** all observations.

6. **Compare** your results with those of other groups of students in your class.

Analyze and Conclude

1. How closely did your results agree with your prediction of how well your building could withstand an earthquake?

2. How did your design compare with those of other teams of students?

3. Which design best stood up to the earthquake? What was important about that design?

INVESTIGATE FURTHER!

EXPERIMENT

After you've had your classroom competition, decide how to improve your design. Redesign, reconstruct, and retest your building. How can you make a tall building earthquake-proof?

The Seismograph

HOW IT Works

Energy from an earthquake travels outward from the focus in all directions, much in the way that energy is released when a pebble is dropped into a pond. Seismic waves travel at different speeds through Earth's crust and upper mantle. P waves are the fastest; S waves are the slowest. These waves are recorded by an instrument called a **seismograph** (sīz′ mə graf).

One of the earliest seismographs used bronze balls to detect earthquake waves.

This Chinese earthquake detector is known as Chang Heng's seismoscope. This early version of a seismograph was used to detect earthquakes. ▼

The dragons on this Chinese earthquake detector clenched the bronze balls in their mouths. When the ground vibrated, one or more balls fell from the dragons' mouths. The balls landed in the mouths of waiting metal toads around the base of the instrument. The noise the balls made when they reached the toads' mouths alerted people that the ground had shaken. The direction from which the waves came was determined by the direction in which the dragons' empty mouths pointed.

A modern seismograph is a device that generally includes a frame (mounted to bedrock), a weight, a pen, and a rotating drum. You built a model of a seismograph on pages B68 and B69. With seismographs, either up-and-down or side-to-side Earth movements can be measured.

A pendulum seismograph consists of a support frame, a heavy weight to which a pen is attached, and a rotating drum. This type of seismograph measures side-to-side Earth movements. A spring seismograph measures up-and-down Earth movements. The drawings on the facing page show you all the parts of these earthquake-recording devices.

Parts of the Seismograph

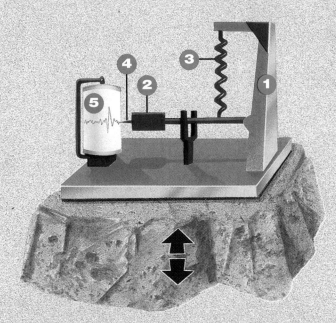

Spring Seismograph

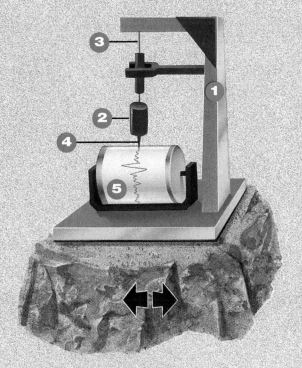

Pendulum Seismograph

1 SUPPORT FRAME
The frame is anchored to solid rock, deep beneath the soil.

2 WEIGHT
The weight of a seismograph is essentially motionless. The magnet reduces the motion of the weight.

3 WIRE OR SPRING
In the spring seismograph, the spring supports the weight. In the pendulum seismograph, the metal wire keeps the weight suspended above the rotating drum.

4 PEN
The pen, which touches the rotating drum, records movements caused by seismic waves.

5 ROTATING DRUM
The drum rotates, or turns, all the time. If there are any movements of Earth, the pen touching the drum records these movements.

INVESTIGATE FURTHER!

RESEARCH

Find out about early seismographs. How are they like modern ones? How are they different from modern ones?

Earthquakes
On the Sea Floor

Tsunamis—What Are They?

You have probably heard the term *tsunami* (tsoo nä'mē). This Japanese word means "harbor wave." You may have heard such waves incorrectly called tidal waves. A **tsunami** has nothing to do with ocean tides. Rather, this seismic sea wave forms when an earthquake occurs on the ocean floor. The earthquake's energy causes the sea floor to move up and down. This movement can produce destructive waves of water. Why are these waves so dangerous?

Most tsunamis are related to the earthquakes that occur around the edges of the Pacific Plate. In these areas massive slabs of rock are being forced down into the mantle. Often, when the plates collide, they lock, allowing energy to build up. Eventually this energy is released as

1 TSUNAMI FORMING
In the open ocean, tsunamis are barely detectable. In deep water, where a tsunami generally forms, the wave's height is only about a meter (about 3 ft).

2 TSUNAMI TRAVELING
In the open ocean, the distance between two crests or troughs can be about 100 km (62.1 mi). A tsunami is often unnoticed in the open ocean, even though it can be traveling close to 800 km/h (496 mph)!

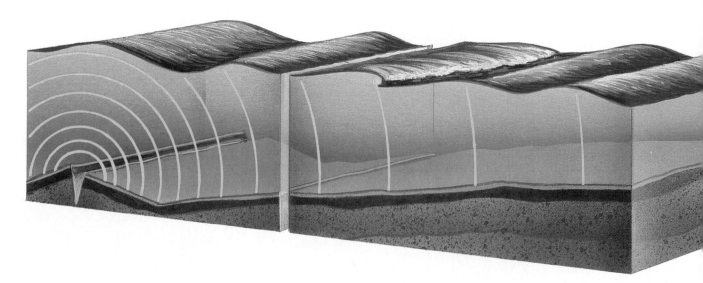

▲ A tsunami

an earthquake, which raises and lowers the nearby ocean floor. This movement sets a tsunami in motion.

Destructive Walls of Water

Most tsunamis are caused by earthquakes. But landslides on the ocean floor and volcanic eruptions can also cause tsunamis. Fortunately, tsunamis only occur about once a year. Study the table on page B78. What was the cause of the 1993 tsunami that began off the coast of Japan?

As with earthquakes, tsunamis cause destruction where they begin as well as along their paths. The tsunami that began with the 1964 Alaskan earthquake, for example, struck the Alaskan coastline and then Vancouver Island in Canada. Waves also struck California and

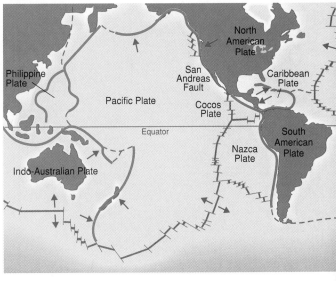

▲ **Tsunamis are common along the shores close to the edges of the Pacific Plate.**

the Hawaiian Islands. The seismic sea waves finally lost their energy at the Japanese coast—over 6,400 km (about 4,000 mi) from their point of origin!

3 TSUNAMI NEARING SHORE
As the wave makes its way toward shore, it slows down due to friction between the advancing water and the ocean floor. But as the water becomes shallower, the height of the wave increases.

4 TSUNAMI STRIKING SHORE
Close to shore a tsunami can reach a height of tens of meters! On March 2, 1933, a tsunami struck the Japanese island of Honshu. It reached a height of 14 m (46 ft).

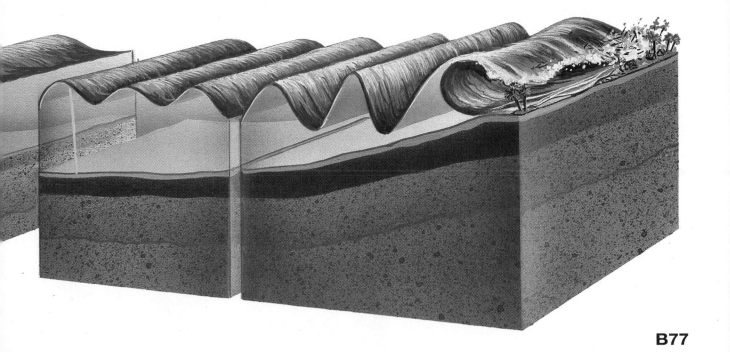

SELECTED TSUNAMIS AND THEIR EFFECTS

Year	Place of Origin	Cause	Height of Water (m)	Deaths
1883	East Indies	volcano	>40 m	>36,000
1896	Japan	earthquake	38 m	26,000
1946	Alaska	earthquake	>30 m	164
1960	Chile	earthquake	6 m	144
1992	Indonesia	earthquake	10 m	71,000
1993	Japan	earthquake	32 m	120

Predicting Tsunamis

Unlike earthquakes and volcanic eruptions, some tsunamis can be predicted. In 1946 the Tsunami Warning System was established to forewarn people in the areas surrounding the Pacific Ocean of these destructive events.

There are two tsunami warning centers in the United States. One center is near Honolulu, Hawaii; the other is just north of Anchorage, in Palmer, Alaska. Scientists at these centers use satellites to gather seismic data from more than 20 countries that border the Pacific Ocean. If earthquakes registering more than about 6.5 on the Richter scale are found, warnings are sent to other centers.

Recall that in the open ocean, tsunamis are hardly detectable at the surface of the water. So in addition to the warning centers, scientists with the National Oceanic and Atmospheric Administration are studying the usefulness of tsunami sensors that rest on the ocean floor. These devices look promising. In water 4,000 to 5,000 m deep, the sensors can detect a change in sea level of less than a millimeter!

Tsunami sensors are flexible metal tubes that are weighted down on the ocean floor. Each tube measures the mass of the water column above it. When a wave passes over the tube, the mass of the water column increases, causing the tube to straighten. After the wave has passed, the tube coils up again. The straightening and coiling of the tubes record changes in water pressure—and the presence of large waves. Such changes can show the presence of tsunamis. ■

Huge waves from a tsunami strike the shore. ▼

Designing For Survival

STS SCIENCE TECHNOLOGY & SOCIETY

Much of the damage done during an earthquake is caused by the earthquake's L waves. Recall that these waves move in two directions—up and down and back and forth. These destructive waves cause the foundations of most buildings to move with the passing waves. The buildings themselves, however, tend to resist the movements.

Because of the damage earthquakes can do, building codes in the western United States and in other earthquake-prone areas of the world have been

CONVENTIONAL FOUNDATION With this foundation, the ground movement is exaggerated on upper floors. The building "drifts," and a lot of damage occurs. Upper floors can collapse onto lower floors.

EARTHQUAKE-RESISTANT FOUNDATION This foundation is built of steel and rubber around columns with lead cores. Since the frame is flexible, the floors can move from side to side, and the building isn't badly damaged.

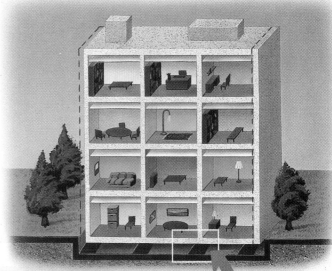

Pillars such as this one support the building and flex during an earthquake. ▶

changed. The new codes deal with the design of new buildings that will help to withstand earthquakes. The building codes also suggest ways to prevent damage in older buildings. Drawings in this resource show some ways that structures are strengthened against earthquakes. ■

Damage to the Golden Gate Freeway, following an earthquake in California in 1989. ▼

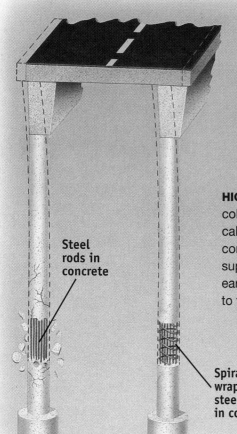

Steel rods in concrete

Spiral-wrapped steel rods in concrete

HIGHWAY SUPPORT The column at the left will probably collapse in an earthquake. The column at the right has vertical steel rods that are spiral-wrapped in steel. This kind of construction could prevent collapse during a quake. Blocks supporting the columns should be able to move with the earthquake. At the same time, they must be firmly anchored to the columns.

═══════ **INVESTIGATION 3** ═══════

1. Compare the effects of an earthquake in which the focus is under the ocean with one in which the focus is under the land.

2. Nearly everyone knows that earthquakes can be dangerous. Explain why some people still choose to live in earthquake-prone areas.

REFLECT & EVALUATE

WORD POWER

aftershock
earthquake
epicenter
fault
focus
magnitude
Richter scale
seismograph
tsunami

 On Your Own
Write a definition for each term in the list.

 With a Partner
Mix up the letters of each term in the list. Provide a clue for each term and challenge your partner to unscramble the terms.

BUILD YOUR PORTFOLIO

Draw a diagram that shows one way an earthquake is produced. Label each part of your diagram.

Analyze Information

What is shown in the drawing below? Describe what might occur at such a location.

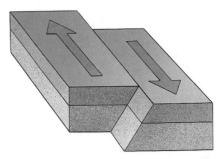

Assess Performance

Work with two or three of your classmates to design and build a model that shows how tsunamis are produced. Describe what each part of your model represents.

Problem Solving

1. Why are strong earthquakes more common on the west coast of the United States than on the east coast?

2. The 1993 earthquake near Los Angeles registered about 7.5 on the Richter scale. The 1964 earthquake near Anchorage, Alaska, registered 8.4 on the Richter scale. Compare the energy released in the two earthquakes.

3. Assume that you live in an area that experiences strong earthquakes. What could you do to protect yourself and your family during an earthquake? What could you do to prepare for an earthquake?

CHAPTER 4

VOLCANOES

Never trust a volcano! Millions of people live near active volcanoes. And over the past 20 years, sudden volcanic eruptions have killed over 28,000 people. Volcanoes have always been unpredictable and dangerous.

Predicting Eruptions

What if scientists could predict the onset of a volcanic eruption? Think of the lives that could be saved by knowing several days in advance that a volcano is about to blow! Barry Voight, a geoscientist at Pennsylvania State University, has come up with a way of making such a prediction.

Voight and his science team have placed monitoring devices on the slopes of Merapi, on the island of Java in Indonesia. Merapi is an active volcano that erupted suddenly in 1930, taking the lives of 1,300 people.

The team uses the monitoring devices and a laser to continually measure the distance to the volcano. Team members who are kilometers away can detect movements of about 2 cm on the surface of the volcano. What do you think such movement on the surface of the volcano tells geoscientists?

Coming Up

◀ Barry Voight and another
geoscientist installing a
monitoring device on Merapi

WHERE DO VOLCANOES OCCUR, AND HOW ARE THEY CLASSIFIED?

Volcanoes form when magma erupts from an opening in Earth's surface. Where are most volcanoes found in relation to tectonic plates? In this investigation you'll locate volcanoes and find out how they are compared and classified.

Activity
Worldwide Eruptions

You can plot volcanic eruptions in the news to figure out how they relate to Earth's tectonic plates.

MATERIALS
- wall map of the world
- table of eruptions
- world almanac
- red map pins
- yellow map pins
- map of tectonic plates
- *Science Notebook*

Procedure

1. Break up into teams of researchers. Each team will research the location of active volcanoes during a six-month period in the last two years. Your teacher will make sure that no two groups are researching the same six months. The goal of all the teams is to collect news articles about active volcanoes throughout the world during the past two years.

2. In your *Science Notebook,* **record** the date of each eruption, the name of the volcano, and the location. Also list whether each volcano is on a spreading ridge, on a plate margin near a descending plate, on a transform fault, or in the middle of a plate. **Record** how each volcano erupted: Was it a quiet lava flow, did it explode, or did it belch heavy clouds of ash?

Step 3

SELECTED MAJOR VOLCANIC ERUPTIONS			
Date	Volcano	Area	Death Toll
79	Vesuvius	Pompeii, Italy	16,000
1169	Etna	Sicily, Italy	15,000
1669	Etna	Sicily, Italy	20,000
1793	Unzen Island	Japan	50,000
1883	Krakatoa	Java, Indonesia	36,000
1902	Pelee	St. Pierre, Martinique	28,000
1919	Kelud	Java, Indonesia	5,500
1980	Saint Helens	Washington State	62
1985	Nevado del Ruis	Armero, Colombia	22,000
1991	Pinatubo	Luzon, Philippines	200
1993	Mayon	Legazpi, Philippines	67

3. Use a world almanac to find the sites of major volcanic activity over the last 500 years.

4. Tack a large world map to your bulletin board. Using the data gathered by the teams, the data from the almanac, and the data in the table, mark the locations of volcanoes. Stick a red map pin on the map at the site of any volcanic eruption; stick a yellow map pin at the site of any active volcano.

5. Throughout the school year, keep adding to your records and to the world map. Record new volcanic activity and new eruptions as they occur. Note how the location of volcanoes is related to Earth's tectonic plates.

Analyze and Conclude

1. How many volcanic eruptions did you find in the news during the six months your team researched? What was the total number of eruptions found by your class during the two-year period?

2. Where on tectonic plates were the volcanoes located?

3. Were any of the volcanic eruptions on a mid-ocean spreading ridge? What kind of an eruption did they have?

4. Hypothesize about the relationship between volcanic eruptions and Earth's tectonic plates.

INVESTIGATE FURTHER!

RESEARCH

Get a world atlas from the library. Look for islands that are in the same locations as mid-ocean ridges. Find out as much as possible about the islands. Are they volcanic? If they are, what kinds of volcanoes are they?

Volcanoes and Plate Tectonics

Volcanoes

What comes to mind when you hear the word *volcano*? Probably you think of a large mountain spewing red-hot lava and other material high into Earth's atmosphere. Some volcanoes are, in fact, towering mountains that throw rock, molten material, dust, and ash into the air. But a **volcano** is *any* opening in Earth's crust through which hot gases, rocks, and melted material erupt.

Have you ever opened a can of cold soda that has been dropped on the floor? Soda probably squirted into the air above the can. More soda bubbled out and flowed down the side of the can. Now, what do you think would happen if you opened a can of warm soda that had been dropped? The release of the warm soda from the can would be *even more* violent. Volcanoes are like cans of soda. Some erupt violently; others have more gentle eruptions.

The high temperatures and pressures deep within Earth can cause rock to melt. This melted rock is called **magma**. Because it's less dense than surrounding material, magma slowly makes its way toward Earth's surface. As it travels toward the surface, the magma melts surrounding material to form a central pipe, which is connected to the magma chamber. Eventually this hot melted material escapes through an opening in the crust called a volcanic vent. When magma reaches Earth's surface, it is called **lava**.

When a volcano erupts, different kinds of materials can be spewed out. Lava is magma that reaches Earth's surface. When lava flows from a volcano, its temperature can be higher than 1,100°C

Structure of an erupting volcano ▼

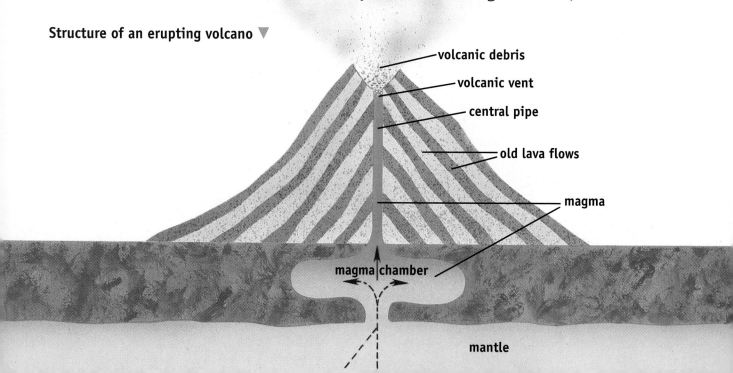

- volcanic debris
- volcanic vent
- central pipe
- old lava flows
- magma
- magma chamber
- mantle

▲ **Mount Tolbackik erupts in former U.S.S.R.**

▲ **Mount Kilauea erupts in Hawaii.**

(2,012°F)! Solid volcanic debris includes bombs, cinders, ash, and dust. Bombs are volcanic rocks the size of a baseball or bigger. Large bombs can weigh nearly 100 metric tons (110 short tons). Volcanic dust and ash, on the other hand, range in size from about 0.25 mm to 0.5 mm (0.009 in. to 0.02 in.) in diameter and can be carried hundreds or thousands of kilometers from a volcano.

Volcanism and Plate Tectonics

Like earthquakes, volcanoes occur along certain plate boundaries. From the map to the right, you can see that many volcanoes occur around the edges of the Pacific Plate in an area that scientists have named the Ring of Fire. Between 500 and 600 active volcanoes make up the region called the Ring of Fire.

Volcanoes in the Ring of Fire were formed in subduction zones. In a subduction zone, plates collide and one plate

descends below the other. The descending plate melts as it descends slowly into the mantle. The magma then rises to the surface, forming a chain of volcanoes near the boundaries of the two plates.

Lava also erupts at divergent plate boundaries. Find the purple faults on the map. These indicate divergent plate boundaries, where new ocean floor is formed as magma wells up between the separating plates.

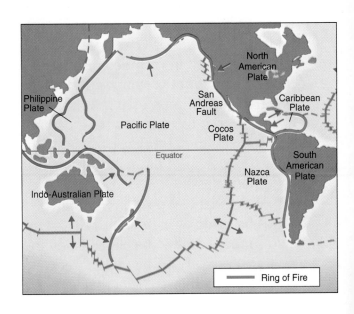

Hundreds of active volcanoes are located in a region known as the Ring of Fire. ▶

B87

CINDER-CONE VOLCANO Paricutín, in Mexico (*left*); drawing of a cinder-cone volcano. Notice the very steep slopes (*below*).

vent

magma

layers of cinders

Classifying Volcanoes

Volcanoes can be classified in different ways. One classification system is based on how often eruptions occur. An *active* volcano is one that erupts constantly. Some volcanoes that make up the Hawaiian Islands are active volcanoes. *Intermittent* volcanoes are those that erupt on a regular basis. Mount Vesuvius, in Italy, is an intermittent volcano. Volcanoes that haven't erupted in a while but could erupt in the near future are called *dormant* volcanoes. Mount Lassen, in the California Cascade Range, is a dormant volcano. Volcanoes that have not erupted in recorded history are classified as *extinct* volcanoes. Mount Kenya, in Africa, is an extinct volcano. Go back to the records you have been keeping from the "Worldwide Eruptions" activity. For each of the volcanoes you have listed, classify it as active, intermittent, or dormant. Would any of the volcanoes be listed as extinct?

Volcanoes can also be classified by the way they erupt. The way they erupt depends on the type of lava that is spewed from the volcano. One kind of lava is highly fluid. Fluid lava erupts quietly. Another kind of lava is very sticky. This sticky lava erupts violently. The kind of lava that pours from the volcano affects the shape of the volcano that is formed. These two pages show the main kinds of volcanoes—cinder cone, shield, and composite-cone—which are based on their shapes.

Cinder-Cone Volcanoes

Cinders are sticky bits of volcanic material that are about the size of peas. A **cinder-cone volcano** is one made of layers of cinders. The cinder cone forms around a central vent containing magma.

These volcanoes are produced by explosive eruptions. Generally, cinder cones are small volcanoes, less than 300 m (984 ft) tall, with very steep slopes. There is usually a bowl-shaped crater. Cinder cones often form in groups. Paricutín, which is a dormant volcano just west of Mexico City, and Stromboli, a very active volcano off the coast of Italy, are cinder-cone volcanoes.

Shield Volcanoes

Shield volcanoes form when lava flows quietly from a crack in Earth's crust. What kind of lava do you think makes up shield volcanoes? Because of the composition of the lava, shield volcanoes are large mountains that have very gentle slopes. Mauna Loa, the largest volcano on Earth, is a shield volcano. Mauna Loa, which is a part of the island of Hawaii, towers over 4,100 m (13,448 ft) above sea level. The rest—about 5,000 m (about 16,400 ft)—of this vast volcano is below the waters of the Pacific Ocean.

vent

magma

layers of lava flows

COMPOSITE-CONE VOLCANO Mount Fuji, in Japan (*top*); a drawing of a composite volcano. This type of volcano has steep slopes near its top and gentle slopes near its base (*bottom*).

Composite-Cone Volcanoes

Composite-cone volcanoes are those that form when explosive eruptions of sticky lava alternate with quieter eruptions of volcanic rock bits. Composite cones are also called stratovolcanoes. A composite cone has very steep slopes near its top but gentle slopes closer to its base.

Composite cones are the most explosive of all volcanoes. Their eruptions often occur without warning and can be very destructive. Mount Vesuvius, a once-dormant volcano in Italy, erupted in A.D. 79 and killed thousands of residents in Pompeii and nearby cities. This same volcano still erupts from time to time. You will learn more about Mount Vesuvius on page B92. ■

vent

layers of lava flows

magma chamber

SHIELD VOLCANO Mauna Loa (*top*); a drawing of a shield volcano. Notice the very gentle slopes (*bottom*).

B89

Surtsey

▲ Surtsey, a young volcanic island, begins to form.

▲ Living things begin to populate the new island of Surtsey.

In 1963 off the southern coast of Iceland, a sailor on a fishing boat observed a pillar of smoke in the distance. He ran to alert his captain that he had spotted a ship that was on fire. Soon the odor of sulfur filled the salty air. The crew of the fishing vessel measured the water's temperature. It was much warmer than usual. The captain soon informed his crew that the smoke in the distance wasn't a burning ship at all. The smoke and fire signaled that one of the youngest volcanic islands on Earth was beginning to rise from the icy waters. Named after the Norse god Surtur, a giant who bore fire from the sea, Surtsey started to form

as lava spewed from a long, narrow rift on the ocean floor.

Within a couple of weeks, an island nearly half a kilometer wide rose about 160 m (528 ft) above the water's surface. And after spewing lava, gases, and bits of rock debris from its vent for almost four years, Surtsey became inactive—geologically, that is. Scientists then had Surtsey designated as a nature preserve in order to study how living things inhabit a newly formed area. Surtsey is now home to 27 species of plants and animals. Among the first organisms to inhabit the island were plants called sea rockets. Seeds from faraway places were carried to the island by

B90

birds and the wind. A few varieties of grasses and mosses painted colorful splotches against the black rock of the island. In the spring, seals now crawl up the black beaches to have their young.

Few people are allowed to visit this volcanic island. The Surtsey Research Council allows only a few scientists to visit the island to study the living things growing there. The impact of the few human beings that visit the island is very small. Only natural forces, such as wind and rain, have acted upon the land and its inhabitants. Erosion has shrunk the island to about three fourths of its original size. Unless it erupts again, the effects of wind and water will eventually make Surtsey disappear. ∎

INVESTIGATE FURTHER!

RESEARCH

In 1973 a volcanic eruption occurred on Heimaey, an island off the southern coast of Iceland. Find out how much destruction was done as a result of this eruption. Look also for ways that the eruption benefited the island. Compare the eruption on Heimaey with the eruption on Surtsey.

SCIENCE IN LITERATURE

SURTSEY:
THE NEWEST PLACE
ON EARTH
by Kathryn Lasky
Photographs by Christopher G. Knight
Hyperion Books for Children, 1992

During the 20 years following the eruption of Surtsey, only about 100 people have been allowed to visit this laboratory of nature. Author-and-photographer team Kathryn Lasky and Christopher Knight are two of the select few who have visited Surtsey.

In the book *Surtsey: The Newest Place on Earth*, you can examine more than 40 color photographs recording Surtsey's formation. In addition to the fascinating photos, author Kathryn Lasky has paired the story of Surtsey with selections from ancient Icelandic mythology. These myths reveal that the people of Iceland have witnessed mid-ocean volcanism for thousands of years.

Mount Vesuvius

ITALY

MOUNT VESUVIUS

TIME Capsule

Over the past 2,000 years or so, Mount Vesuvius, a cinder-cone volcano in southern Italy, has erupted about 50 times. Before its eruption in A.D. 79, Vesuvius was a picturesque cone-shaped mountain, towering over 1,000 m (3,300 ft) above the Bay of Naples. Vineyards and orchards crept nearly halfway up the mountain's slopes. Most historians think that very few people knew that Vesuvius was a volcano—until the fateful morning of August 24 in the year A.D. 79.

During the early morning hours of that day, an earthquake rumbled through the area. By early afternoon loud thunder ripped through the air, and red-hot ash rained from the skies. Within 24 hours the twin Roman cities of Pompeii and Herculaneum were destroyed.

In Pompeii more than 2,000 people were buried beneath about 5 to 8 m (16 to 26 ft) of volcanic ash. Because the ash was so hot and fell so quickly, it preserved many of the city's residents doing what they normally did in their day-to-day lives. By studying the remains of people, animals, utensils, and decorations found in Pompeii, archaeologists have learned a lot about the people who lived at this time. Archaeologists are scientists who study ancient cultures by digging up the evidence of human life from the past.

The city of Herculaneum, which was several kilometers from Pompeii, met its fate not from the volcanic ash but from a mudflow. A mudflow is a mixture of wet materials that rushes down a mountainside and destroys everything in its path. Volcanologists, or scientists who study volcanoes, think that flowing hot volcanic debris swept over the city and covered it to depths of over 20 m (66 ft)!

The eruption of Mount Vesuvius in A.D. 79 is probably most famous because

Cast of man buried by the eruption of Mount Vesuvius (*far left*); nuts buried and preserved by the eruption (*left*)

it perfectly preserved the people and customs of ancient Rome. However, it was not the last nor the worst eruption in the area. In the summer of 1631, earthquakes once again shook the area. By winter, molten rock filled the volcano. On December 16, 1631, ash was spewing from the mountain. By the next day, red-hot lava raced down the volcano's slopes. The destructive toll of this eruption included 15 villages. At least 4,000 people and 6,000 animals died.

Since the 1631 eruption of Mount Vesuvius, the volcano has erupted every 15 to 40 years. The ash and rock fragments have made the soil very fertile. Farmers successfully grow grapes, citrus fruits, carnations, beans, and peas in this region. But the threat of losing it all to the volcano is always there. ■

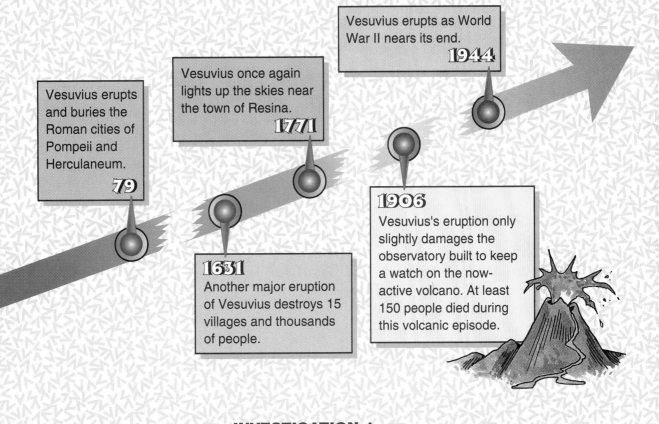

Vesuvius erupts as World War II nears its end.
1944

Vesuvius once again lights up the skies near the town of Resina.
1771

Vesuvius erupts and buries the Roman cities of Pompeii and Herculaneum.
79

1631
Another major eruption of Vesuvius destroys 15 villages and thousands of people.

1906
Vesuvius's eruption only slightly damages the observatory built to keep a watch on the now-active volcano. At least 150 people died during this volcanic episode.

INVESTIGATION 1

1. Describe how most volcanoes form.

2. Make a chart that compares and contrasts cinder cones, shield volcanoes, and composite cones. In your chart, include a sketch of each type of volcano. Label the parts of each volcano.

HOW DO VOLCANIC ERUPTIONS AFFECT EARTH?

In March 1980, a strong earthquake rocked Mount St. Helens, in the state of Washington. For the next two months steam and ash blew out. Then in May, the volcano exploded with great violence. In this investigation you'll find out what you can expect before, during, and after a volcanic eruption.

Activity

Volcanoes You Can Eat!

How is an erupting volcano like a pot of cooking oatmeal? Volcanoes erupt because liquids, solids, and gases are forced out of a hole, called a vent. Can you see a vent in a pot of oatmeal?

Procedure

1. Use the measuring cup to **measure** quick oats and water.

2. Put the oats and water into a saucepan and mix together.

3. Place the saucepan on a hot plate and set the hot plate on *Medium High*.

Step 4

4. After the hot plate has warmed up, stir the oats and water constantly for one minute.

5. Carefully observe the top surface of the oatmeal as it cooks. Record your observations in your *Science Notebook*.

6. After one minute, remove the oatmeal from the heat and turn off the hot plate.

Analyze and Conclude

1. What did you observe on the surface of the oatmeal as it cooked?

2. How is cooking oatmeal like an erupting volcano? How is it different?

UNIT PROJECT LINK

Have you ever dreamed of living on your own island paradise? Locate the Ring of Fire on a map and identify those islands created by volcanic activity. Predict where future volcanic islands might rise out of the ocean; indicate these areas on your map. Draw a small picture of your island paradise and describe where you think your island will emerge.

Mount Pinatubo

THE PHILIPPINES

Mount Pinatubo, which towers over 1,900 m (6,232 ft) above sea level, is only one of about 13 active volcanoes in the Philippines. This volcano, which is located on the island of Luzon, is a composite cone. At times when it erupts, there is a sticky lava flow. At other times a combination of ash, dust, and other volcanic rock bits erupt from the volcano.

Mount Pinatubo and the other volcanoes in the Philippines formed as a result of tectonic activity. The Philippine Islands are a part of the Ring of Fire.

You already know that at some convergent plate boundaries, one oceanic plate collides with another oceanic plate. At such boundaries, one plate goes down deep into Earth's mantle. As the plate is dragged down, it bends, and a deep canyon, or ocean trench, forms. As this oceanic plate descends into the asthenosphere, parts of the plate melt, forming magma. The magma then rises and forms a chain of volcanoes called **island arcs**. The islands that make up the Philippines are a mature island arc system that formed long ago when two oceanic plates collided.

There She Blows!

After being dormant for over six centuries, Mount Pinatubo began to erupt in mid-June of 1991. As the eruption began, brilliant lightning bolts colored the skies above the volcano. Within minutes, these same skies were black because of the enormous amounts of ash, dust, and gases that spurted from the mountain. Scientists estimate that the mountain's violent eruption had a force equal to that of 2,000 to 3,000 exploding atomic bombs! The ash clouds produced by the eruption polluted the air so much that astronauts out in space in the space shuttle could not get a clear view of Earth's surface!

This period of volcanic activity lasted for several months and stopped in early September 1991. The first eruption

Two oceanic plates colliding at their boundaries ▼

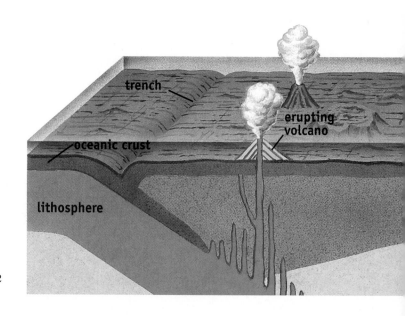

trench

erupting volcano

oceanic crust

lithosphere

destroyed about 42,000 houses and nearly 100,000 acres of farmland. Over 900 people died. Much of the damage and many of the deaths were caused by flowing mud and hot volcanic material. Also, masses of gas, ash, and igneous rock called pumice covered many villages at and near the base of Mount Pinatubo.

The cause of the 1991 eruption of Mount Pinatubo is not completely understood. It is likely that many months prior to the eruption, magma began forcing its way up through the lithosphere. Slowly the magma made its way toward the surface. As it snaked along its path, the magma increased temperatures and pressures beneath the mountain. In some places the magma crept into cracks in the bedrock, causing the bedrock to swell. On June 15, 1991, the mountain erupted, sending clouds of gases and tons of lava to Earth's surface.

Mount Pinatubo's Warning Signs

Earthquakes and volcanoes are more common in some parts of the world than

JUNE 19-27, 1991

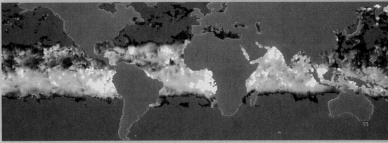

AUGUST 8-14, 1991

▲ **Effect of the eruption of Mount Pinatubo. The yellow band shows how volcanic debris travels around the globe and extends over time.**

in others. Both are closely related to the movements of tectonic plates. Scientists monitor earthquake- and volcano-prone areas for changes. But the exact time of volcanic eruptions can be difficult to predict accurately. Fortunately, in the case of Mount Pinatubo, the mountain "cooperated." There were many warnings of its explosive 1991 eruption.

First, there was an earthquake that shook the area in July 1990. There is

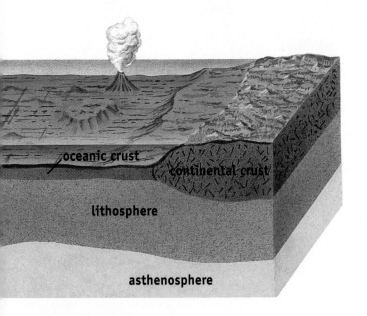

oceanic crust

continental crust

lithosphere

asthenosphere

INVESTIGATE FURTHER!

RESEARCH

Find out about another famous volcano in the Philippines called Mount Mayon. Where is it located? How do you think this volcano formed? When did it last erupt? What kind of volcano is it?

◀ **Clouds and gases rise from Mount Pinatubo.**

the 1991 eruption. Its lava dome, a bulge that is produced when sticky lava is slowly squeezed from a volcano's vent, had doubled in size in a little over two months!

Because the volcano gave these warning signs, many lives were saved. For several months before the explosion, scientists explained what the mountain was doing and urged people to leave the area. Over 200,000 people had been safely evacuated before the explosion.

What Goes Up Must Come Down— But When?

Before the eruption, instruments aboard weather satellites monitored the atmosphere above the volcano. These instruments were looking for increases in the amount of sulfur dioxide in the air around the composite cone. About two weeks before the explosion, the amount of sulfur dioxide was ten times what it

often a relationship between earthquake activity and later volcanic activity. In April 1991, small clouds of smoke and ash were forced from cracks along the mountain's slopes. These clouds prompted earth scientists from the Philippines and the United States to more closely monitor the majestic Pinatubo.

Watching Pinatubo

Two kinds of measuring devices—seismometers and tiltmeters—were put into place near the mountain and then connected to computers. A **seismometer** is an instrument that detects Earth's movements. These movements can indicate that a volcano is preparing to blow its top! A tiltmeter measures any change in the slope of an area. Installing these devices allowed scientists to note any bulges in the mountain's slopes. Such bulges indicate the presence of magma and/or gases welling up into the volcano. In fact, Mount Pinatubo did bulge before

Evacuation of people before the eruption of Mount Pinatubo ▶

had been the month before. This increase was another warning that Mount Pinatubo might erupt.

These same instruments measured the amount of sulfur dioxide that had been spewed out into the air during the eruption. About 15 to 20 million tons of this gas blew nearly 40 km (about 25 mi) into the air! This gas combined with other gases in the air and formed a thin layer of sulfuric acid droplets that circled the globe within about three weeks.

Mount Pinatubo, like other active volcanoes, is a source of pollution. The dust, gases, and ash spewed out in 1991 had several effects on Earth and its atmosphere. First, vivid sunsets colored the skies in many places far removed from the Philippines.

Second, the sulfuric acid droplets remained above the planet for a few years following the eruption. The droplets reflected back into space about 2 percent of the Sun's energy that normally reached Earth's surface. This in turn led to a global cooling of about 1°C (1.2°F). This short period of cooling reversed a global warming trend for a short time. The warming

▲ Sunset after the 1991 eruption of Mount Pinatubo

trend is caused by the collection of gases that trap the Sun's heat. This effect, called the greenhouse effect, is the result of natural climatic changes and human activities, such as burning fossil fuels and cutting down forests.

Another effect of the 1991 eruption of Mount Pinatubo is that the 30 to 40 million tons of sulfuric acid added to the air may speed up the breakdown of Earth's ozone layer. The ozone layer in the upper atmosphere protects you and Earth's other inhabitants from harmful solar rays. ■

━━━━━━━ **INVESTIGATION 2** ━━━━━━━

1. Using Mount Pinatubo as your example, explain how volcanic eruptions can have long-term effects on the planet.

2. Describe some of the events that may occur and some measurements that may be taken to alert scientists to a coming volcanic eruption.

IN WHAT OTHER PLACES CAN VOLCANOES OCCUR?

So far, you have learned that volcanoes can occur along mid-ocean ridges and where one tectonic plate is descending under another. In this investigation you'll explore two other kinds of places where volcanoes can occur.

MATERIALS
- metric ruler
- map of the Hawaiian Islands, showing volcanoes
- calculator
- *Science Notebook*

Activity

How Hawaii Formed

Geologists have a hypothesis that magma rising from a large chamber of molten rock—called a hot spot— deep below the Pacific Plate has built the volcanic islands that make up the state of Hawaii. In this activity you'll examine some of their evidence.

Procedure

1. **Measure** the distance between the center of the island of Hawaii and the center of each of the other islands. **Record** this information in your *Science Notebook.* Use the map scale to find out how far apart the centers are.

2. The table on this page tells you the estimated age of the rock on each island. **Record** the youngest island and the oldest island.

3. **Make a chart** that shows the age difference between Hawaii and each of the other islands.

THE HAWAIIAN ISLANDS	
Island	**Estimated Age of Rock**
Maui	1.63 million years
Molokai	1.84 million years
Oahu	2.9 million years
Kauai	5.1 million years
Hawaii	375,000 years
Lanai	1.28 million years
Niihau	5.5 million years
Kahoolawe	1.03 million years

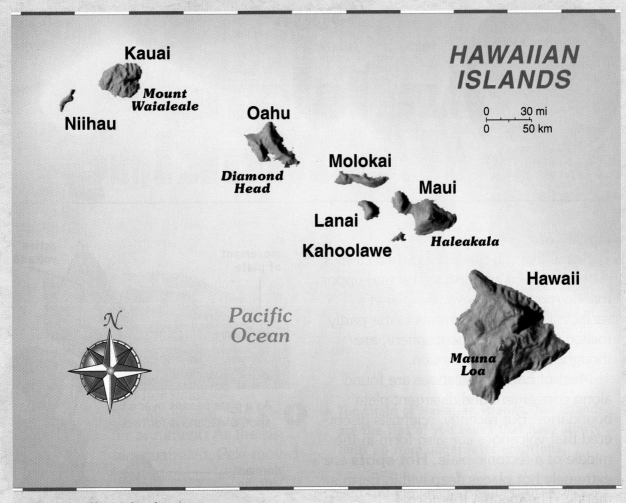

HAWAIIAN ISLANDS

Kauai

Mount Waialeale

Niihau

Oahu

Diamond Head

Molokai

Maui

Lanai

Kahoolawe

Haleakala

Hawaii

Pacific Ocean

N

Mauna Loa

| 0 | 30 mi |
| 0 | 50 km |

▲ The Hawaiian Islands

Analyze and Conclude

1. Based on your measurements, how far apart are the Hawaiian Islands?

2. Which island is the youngest? Which is the oldest?

3. If the hot spot under the islands stayed in the same place and the Pacific Plate moved over it, the hot spot may have created one island after another. In which direction does this show the Pacific Plate moving?

4. Based on the dates of formation of Hawaii and Kauai, what was the speed of the plate's movement?

5. Would you say that the Pacific Plate moves at a nearly constant speed, or does its speed change from time to time? What evidence supports your conclusion?

INVESTIGATE FURTHER!

· · · · · · · · · · · · · · · · · ·

RESEARCH

Look at a map of Earth's surface features. Observe the northwestward underwater extension of the Hawaiian Islands. Notice that there is an abrupt northward bend where the Hawaiian chain meets the Emperor Seamount chain. What do you think this bend means?

Using Robots
to Investigate Volcanoes

What has eight legs and a "nerve cord" that sends and receives messages, is over 3 m (9.84 ft) tall, weighs about 772 kg (1,698 lb), and costs nearly $2 million? Give up? It's Dante, a series of robots designed by computer scientists at Carnegie-Mellon University, in Pittsburgh, Pennsylvania.

Dante II exploring a volcano in Anchorage, Alaska ▼

Dante was named after a fourteenth-century poet who wrote a poem in which he spends some time traveling through fiery regions deep within Earth. During a part of his mythical journey, Dante is led by a ghost named Virgil. Because the scientists send their robots into the fiery depths of volcanoes, they thought it appropriate to name the robots Dante. A transporter robot called Virgil carries Dante along some stretches of its journeys.

The first version of Dante was designed to help volcanologists explore one of the most active volcanoes on Earth—Mount Erebus, a smoldering 3,790-m (12,431-ft) volcano on Antarctica. A kink in one of the robot's cables, however, stopped the robot from going deeper than 6 m (about 20 ft) into the volcano. Although it couldn't complete its mission, Dante proved that it could tackle similar future assignments.

Dante II made its debut in Anchorage, Alaska, where scientists used this improved robot to explore Alaska's active Mount Spurr. The robot could descend slowly but surely 100 m (330 ft) into the volcano. It was able to produce a three-dimensional map of the rugged terrain of the crater's floor. Dante II could also collect and analyze gases being emitted from the volcano. Scientists used the information to infer that Mount Spurr will probably remain dormant for some time.

The Amazing Dante II, A Volcano-Exploring Robot

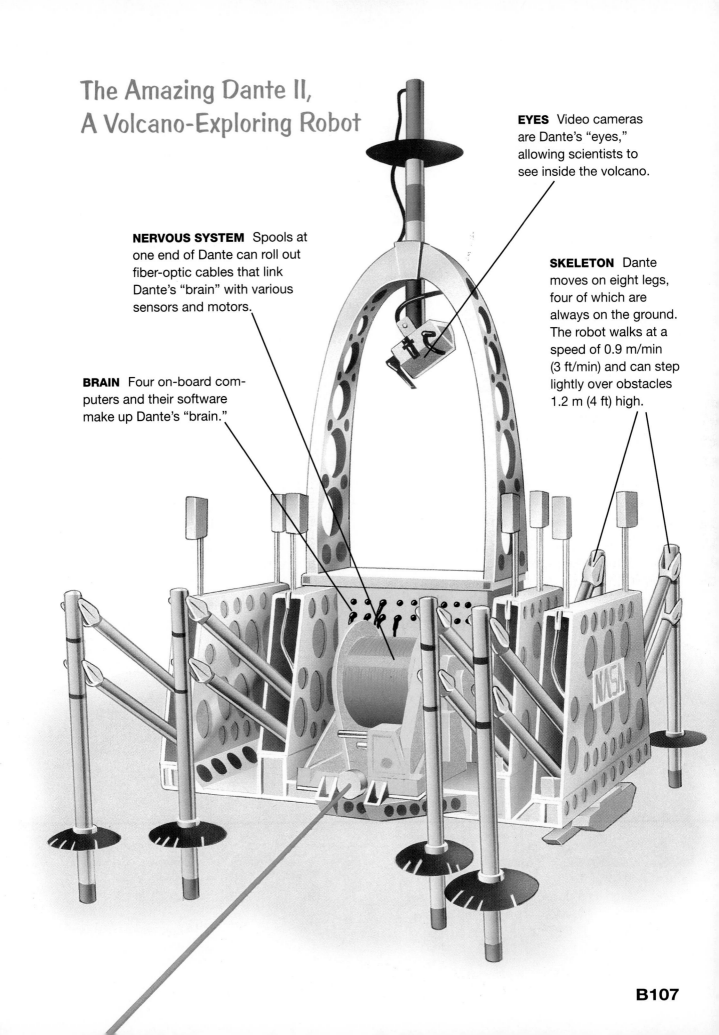

EYES Video cameras are Dante's "eyes," allowing scientists to see inside the volcano.

NERVOUS SYSTEM Spools at one end of Dante can roll out fiber-optic cables that link Dante's "brain" with various sensors and motors.

SKELETON Dante moves on eight legs, four of which are always on the ground. The robot walks at a speed of 0.9 m/min (3 ft/min) and can step lightly over obstacles 1.2 m (4 ft) high.

BRAIN Four on-board computers and their software make up Dante's "brain."

Great Rift Valley of Africa

Rifting

What happens if you slowly pull on some silicon putty? The putty stretches, sags, and often breaks. The process of rifting is similar to your stretching the putty.

Rifting is a process that occurs at divergent plate boundaries. As two plates separate, hot magma in the asthenosphere oozes upward to fill the newly formed gap. In general, rifting occurs along mid-ocean ridges deep beneath the oceans. Rifting along mid-ocean ridges leads to the process of sea-floor spreading. Some rifting, however, occurs where two continental plates are moving apart. When rifting occurs on land, the continental crust breaks up, or splits. Study the drawings on these two pages. What

eventually forms when rifting occurs in continental crust?

The Great African Rift System

Over the past 25 million to 30 million years, continental rifting has been pulling eastern Africa apart—at the rate of several centimeters per decade. Jokes a Djibouti geologist, "[We are] Africa's fastest-growing nation!" Three rifts—the East African Rift, one in the Gulf of Aden, and a third in the Red Sea—form a 5,600-km-long (3,472-mi-long) system known as the Great Rift Valley. The place where the three rift systems meet is called the Afar Triangle, named after the people who live in the region.

The Great Rift Valley is the place

2 The crust pulls apart, faults open, and blocks of crust fall inward. Volcanoes begin to erupt. A rift valley forms.

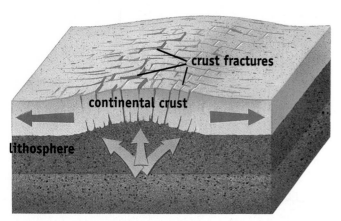

1 Magma produced by Earth's mantle rises through the crust, lifts it up, and causes fractures in the crust.

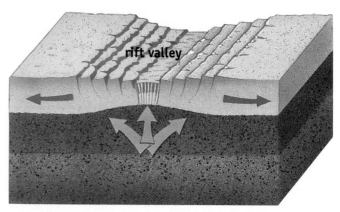

where humans had their first encounters with volcanoes. In fact, it is because of volcanic eruptions that anthropologists today are finding very old human remains. Some human ancestors living in the Afar region of Africa were buried under the volcanic debris of an eruption that occurred millions of years ago! Their fossil remains continue to be unearthed and provide important information about where early humans lived.

Found along the Great Rift Valley are some of the world's oldest volcanoes—including Mount Kenya and Mount Kilimanjaro. Mount Kilimanjaro, a volcano that towers nearly 5,900 m (19,352 ft) above the surrounding land, is Africa's highest peak.

Rifting along the Great Rift Valley—which runs through Mozambique, Zambia, Zaire, Tanzania, Uganda, Kenya, and Sudan, up into the Ethiopian highlands and down into the Djibouti coastal plains—has produced some of Earth's deepest lakes as well as some of the high-

▲ **Mount Kilimanjaro, one of Earth's oldest volcanoes**

est volcanic mountains. Lake Tanganyika, the longest freshwater lake on Earth, is the second deepest lake in the world. It formed millions of years ago when two tectonic plates shifted horizontally.

All along the Great Rift Valley, as with any rift zone, earthquakes and volcanoes are common. Study the map on page B110. Notice that along the East African Rift, the Somali Plate is moving away from

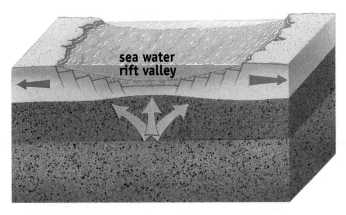

3 The rift valley widens, allowing sea water to fill the basin that has formed.

4 A new rift begins in the middle of the ocean basin that was formed. This rift is known as a mid-ocean ridge.

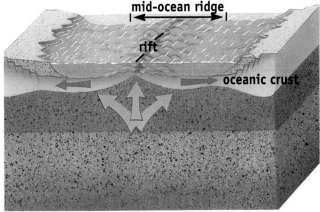

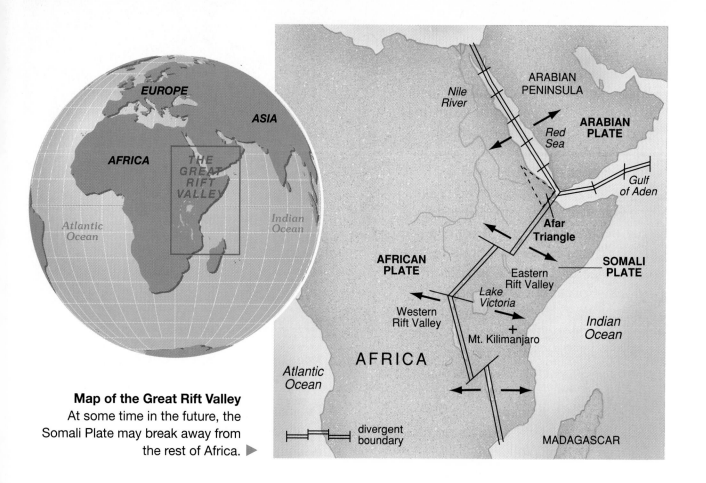

Map of the Great Rift Valley
At some time in the future, the Somali Plate may break away from the rest of Africa. ▶

the African Plate. Along the Gulf of Aden arm of the rift, the Somali Plate is moving southwestward relative to the Arabian Plate. How might this area look 30 million years from now if rifting continues?

As with most volcanic areas, fertile soils cover much of the land in the Great Rift Valley. In Kenya, for example, rich red soils blanket the land. Trona, a min-eral in the local volcanic ash, is used to make glass and detergents.

Near the Afar Triangle, where Earth's crust is only 25 km (15.5 mi) thick, steam from the many volcanoes spouts into the air. Someday, perhaps, the volcanoes of the rift system will provide electricity from geothermal energy to Africa's millions of residents. ■

INVESTIGATION 3

1. Volcanoes occur on Earth's surface—the crust. Yet scientists study volcanoes to find out about the planet's mantle. Explain why.

2. Using the Hawaiian Islands as an example, describe how volcanic islands can occur in places other than at the boundaries of tectonic plates.

REFLECT & EVALUATE

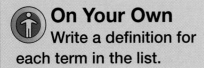

caldera
cinder-cone volcano
composite-cone volcano
hot spot
island arc
lava
magma
rifting
seismometer
shield volcano
volcano

On Your Own
Write a definition for each term in the list.

With a Partner
Make a labeled drawing or model of one of the three types of volcanoes.

Search through magazines and newspapers. Make photocopies of pictures of each of the three kinds of volcanoes.

Analyze Information

Use the drawing below to help explain how the Hawaiian Islands show the direction in which the Pacific Plate is moving.

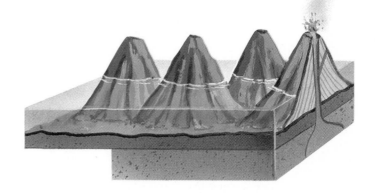

Assess Performance

Locate the Hawaiian Islands on a world map. Then locate them on a tectonic-plates map. Name the plate on which they are located and the direction in which the plate is moving.

Problem Solving

1. How are volcanoes on spreading ridges and rift zones different from those above descending edges of ocean plates?

2. On a map of Earth's tectonic plates, show where volcanoes are most likely to occur. Identify five active volcanoes throughout the world.

3. Explain how a satellite map could demonstrate that a volcano has erupted. How might that map change in a couple of months?

Throughout this unit you've investigated questions related to the changing Earth. How will you use what you've learned and share that information with others? Here are some ideas...

Hold a Big Event
to Share Your Unit Project

Imagine that you live in a part of the world where earthquakes occur frequently or where a volcano erupts from time to time. You are part of a team that is developing a guide—Preparing for an Earthquake and for Volcanic Activity. Your guide should give people information on protecting themselves against earthquakes and volcanic eruptions. It should prepare people for emergency measures, such as evacuation procedures. Be sure to include maps, tables, and other ways to communicate ideas clearly.

Experiment

Plan a long-term project based on this unit. Monitor newspapers and/or news broadcasts for at least two months. Record reported incidents of earthquakes and volcanoes. On a world map, place colored labels at those sites that experience seismic or volcanic activity. Note any patterns in the incidents: on fault lines, near the Ring of Fire, and so on. What conclusions can you draw about geologically active areas? What predictions would you make on the basis of your conclusions?

Take Action

If areas in your state are geologically active, find out what kinds of structures and industries are nearby. What safety precautions are in place in the event of earthquakes or volcanic activity? Write your local newspaper or government officials. Express your views about the quality of safety standards at these sites. Report your recommendations and any responses to your class.

SCIENCE Handbook

THINK LIKE A SCIENTIST

You don't have to be a professional scientist to act and think like one. Thinking like a scientist mostly means using common sense. It also means learning how to test your ideas in a careful way.

In other words, *you* can think like a scientist.

Make a Hypothesis

Plan and Do a Test

Make Observations

To think like a scientist, you should learn as much as you can by observing things around you. Everything you hear and see is a clue about how the natural world works.

Ask a Question

Look for patterns. You'll get ideas and ask questions like these:

- Do all birds eat the same seeds?

- How does the time that the Sun sets change from day to day?

Make a Guess Called a Hypothesis

If you have an idea about why or how something happens, make an educated guess, or *hypothesis*, that you can test. For example, let's suppose that your hypothesis about the sunset time is that it changes by one minute each day.

Plan and Do a Test

Plan how to test your hypothesis. Your plan would need to consider some of these problems:

- How will you measure the time that the Sun sets?

- Will you measure the time every day?

- For how many days or weeks do you need to measure?

Record and Analyze What Happens

When you test your idea, you need to observe carefully and write down, or record, everything that happens. When you finish collecting data, you may need to do some calculations with it. For example, you might want to calculate how much the sunset time changes in a week or a month.

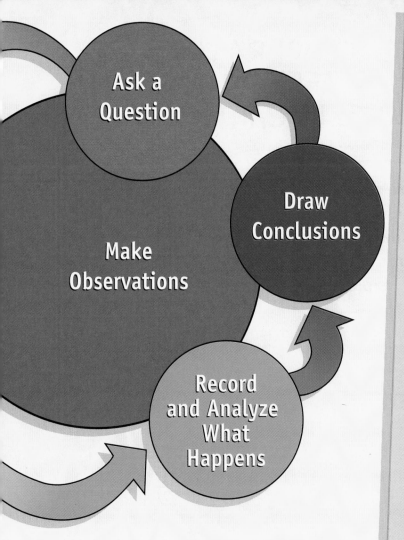

Ask a
Question

Draw
Conclusions

Make
Observations

Record
and Analyze
What
Happens

Draw Conclusions

Whatever happens in a test, think about all the reasons for your results. For example, you might wonder what causes the time of sunset to change. You might also ask when the earliest and latest sunsets occur during the year. Sometimes this thinking leads to a new hypothesis.

If the time of the sunset changes by one minute each day, think about what else the data shows you. Can you predict the time that the Sun will set one month from now?

PRACTICE SCIENTIFIC REASONING SKILLS

To think like a scientist, you need to practice certain ways of thinking.

Always check for yourself.
Always ask, "How do I really know it's true?" Be willing to find out for yourself.

Be honest and careful about what you observe.
It's easy to only look for the results you expect. It's harder to see the unexpected. But unexpected results lead scientists to ask more questions. They also provide information on how things work.

Don't be afraid to be wrong.
Based on their observations, scientists make many hypotheses. Not all of these hypotheses turn out to be correct. But scientists can learn from wrong "guesses," because even wrong guesses result in information that leads to knowledge.

Keep an open mind about possible explanations.
Make sure to think about all the reasons why something might have happened. Consider all the explanations that you can think of.

> ### DOES THE TEMPERATURE OF A LIQUID AFFECT HOW MUCH SOLUTE IT CAN HOLD?

> Here's an example of an everyday problem and how thinking like a scientist can help you explore it.

"I can't believe it."

"It's true."

"It's impossible! Ten?"

"That's right."

"A cup of herbal tea can't hold ten teaspoons of sugar."

"My mother's does," replied Mark. "She likes it sweet."

"I'll bet most of the sugar just sinks to the bottom of the cup," Nita asserted. "Doesn't it?"

"No, it doesn't," Mark said. "Would I lie to you?"

"Listen," Nita said, "Ms. Cobb's been teaching us about solutions. I'll bet if I asked her she'd say it's impossible."

Make Observations

Ask a Question

Nita explained the issue to Ms. Cobb and the other students. She asked Ms. Cobb to give her opinion, but she wouldn't. She simply asked the class what they thought. Some students thought it was possible, others thought it was impossible. Ms. Cobb suggested that the class figure out a way to find the answer.

Ms. Cobb invited the students to come up with questions that expressed the problem they want to solve. Two of the questions were:

How much sugar can a cup of herbal tea hold?

Can hot water dissolve more sugar than cold water can?

Nita and Mark thought the second question was more interesting because it applied to more things—like coffee and lemonade. They were not sure what the answer to this question would be. But it was the kind of question that would tell them more about the nature of solutions.

> Scientific investigations usually begin with something that you have noticed or read about. As you think about what you already know, you'll discover some ideas that you're not sure about. This will help you to ask the question that you really want to answer.

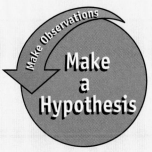

Make a Hypothesis

Mark and Nita talked the problem over. Mark told Nita that his mother drank her herbal tea very hot; she always waited until the water was boiling violently before pouring it into her cup. "Maybe," Nita said, "if the water wasn't so hot, it would hold less sugar." Mark agreed that this was possible. But he wasn't sure.

Mark and Nita had a hunch that the hotter water is, the more solute, such as sugar, the water will hold. They came up with a hypothesis, a statement of what they thought was true. Their hypothesis was "The hotter the water, the more sugar it will dissolve."

Nita and Mark got a few heat-proof glass beakers, a cup measure, and thermometers. Ms. Cobb got 1-teaspoon measuring spoons and a bowl of sugar from the school cafeteria. She also borrowed several hotplates. Ms. Cobb reviewed the test procedure that Mark and Nita had planned.

> When you use what you have observed to suggest a possible answer to your question, you are making a *hypothesis*. Be sure that your hypothesis is an idea that you can test somehow. If you can't think of an experiment or a model to test your hypothesis, try changing it. Sometimes it's better to make a simpler, clearer hypothesis that answers only part of your question.

Plan and Do a Test

Make Observations

Mark and Nita knew they'd have to keep track of the different water temperatures in each beaker. They knew they'd have to put the same amount of water in each beaker. They would also have to keep track of how many teaspoons of sugar went into each beaker.

Nita knew that water boiled at 100 degrees Celsius (°C). So the beaker with the hottest water should be at this temperature. Another beaker could have water at 70°C; a third might have water at 40°C.

Mark suggested that they have a fourth beaker containing a cup of cold water at about 5°C—water whose temperature was close to freezing. This beaker would serve as their control. The control in this experiment would allow Mark and Nita to test the effect of heat on water's ability to dissolve sugar.

Ms. Cobb set up four water baths at the temperatures they agreed upon. Each was kept at a constant temperature. Each water bath had a thermometer in it.

One way to try out your hypothesis is to use a test called an experiment. When you plan an experiment, be sure that it helps you to answer your question. Even when you plan, things can happen that make the experiment confusing or make it not work properly. If this happens, you can change the plan for the experiment, and try again.

Record and Analyze What Happened

Make Observations

Mark and Nita asked two classmates to help them put teaspoons of sugar into the beakers. After each teaspoon of sugar went in, the solution was stirred with a glass stirring rod until the sugar dissolved. Each

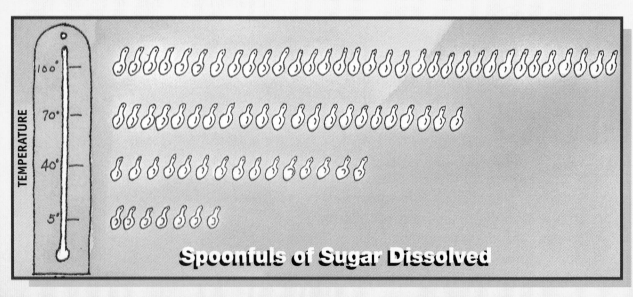

Spoonfuls of Sugar Dissolved

student kept track of the number of teaspoons of sugar that dissolved in it.

At the end of the experiment, each student looked at what he or she had written down. This information was organized in a graph like the one on page H6.

Mark and Nita studied the graph of the data they got during their experiment. They noticed that there was a definite relationship between water temperature and how much sugar could be dissolved in it.

Nita was surprised to see that Mark's mother's tea could really hold a lot more than 10 teaspoons of sugar. She and Mark agreed that people could drink their tea really sweet, unless, that is, they made it with cooler water.

Draw Conclusions
Make Observations

Mark and Nita decided that their test results supported their hypothesis. But they had noticed something odd that had happened in the beaker containing the hottest water. At some point after the water had cooled, a small amount of sugar added to the solution caused many sugar crystals to form.

They told Ms. Cobb about this strange result. Ms. Cobb congratulated them for having created a "supersaturated" solution. She suggested that Mark and Nita might want to plan another experiment to find out more about such solutions.

When you do an experiment, you need to write down, or record, your observations. Some of your observations might be numbers – things that you counted or measured. Your recorded observations are called data. When you record your data, you need to organize it in a way that helps you to understand it. Graphs and tables are helpful ways to organize data. Then think about the information you have collected. Analyze what it tells you.

After you have analyzed your data, you should use what you have learned to draw a conclusion. A conclusion is a statement that sums up what you learned. The conclusion should be about the question you asked. Think about whether the information you have gathered supports your hypothesis or not. If it does, figure out how to check out your idea more thoroughly. Also think about new questions you can ask.

SAFETY

The best way to be safe in the classroom is to use common sense. Prepare yourself for each activity before you start it. Get help from your teacher when there is a problem. Most important of all, pay attention. Here are some other ways that you can stay safe.

Stay Safe From Stains

- Wear protective clothing or an old shirt when you work with messy materials.
- If anything spills, wipe it up or ask your teacher to help you clean it up.

Stay Safe From Flames

- Keep your clothes away from open flames. If you have long or baggy sleeves, roll them up.
- Don't let your hair get close to a flame. If you have long hair, tie it back.

Stay Safe During Cleanup

- Wash up after you finish working.
- Dispose of things in the way that your teacher tells you to.

Stay Safe From Injuries

- Protect your eyes by wearing safety goggles when you are told that you need them.
- Keep your hands dry around electricity. Water is a good conductor of electricity, so you can get a shock more easily if your hands are wet.
- Be careful with sharp objects. If you have to press on them, keep the sharp side away from you.
- Cover any cuts you have that are exposed. If you spill something on a cut, be sure to wash it off immediately.
- Don't eat or drink anything unless your teacher tells you that it's okay.

MOST IMPORTANTLY

If you ever hurt yourself or one of your group members gets hurt, tell your teacher right away.

HAIR Keep it out of the way of a flame.

EYES Wear safety goggles when you are told to.

MOUTH Don't eat or drink **ANYTHING** unless your teacher tells you it's okay.

HANDS Keep your hands dry around electricity. Cover any cuts. Wear gloves when told to. Wash up after you finish.

CLOTHES Keep long sleeves rolled up. Protect yourself from stains. Stay away from open flames.

DON'T MAKE A MESS If you spill something, clean it up right away. When finished with an activity, clean up your work area. Dispose of things in the way your teacher tells you to.

Using a Microscope

A microscope makes it possible to see very small things by magnifying them. Some microscopes have a set of lenses to magnify objects different amounts.

Examine Some Salt Grains

Handle a microscope carefully; it can break easily. Carry it firmly with both hands and avoid touching the lenses.

1. Turn the mirror toward a source of light. **NEVER** use the Sun as a light source.

2. Place a few grains of salt on the slide. Put the slide on the stage of the microscope.

3. While looking through the eyepiece, turn the adjustment knob on the back of the microscope to bring the salt grains into focus.

4. Raise the eyepiece tube to increase the magnification; lower it to decrease magnification.

Using a Calculator

After you've made measurements, a calculator can help you analyze your data. Some calculators have a memory key that allows you to save the result of one calculation while you do another.

Find an Average

The table shows the amount of rain that was collected using a rain gauge in each month of one year. You can use a calculator to help you find the average monthly rainfall.

1. Add the numbers. When you add a series of numbers, you don't need to press the equal sign until the last number is entered. Just press the plus sign after you enter each number (except the last one).

2. If you make a mistake while you are entering numbers, try to erase your mistake by pushing the clear entry (CE) key or the clear (C) key. Then you can continue entering the rest of the numbers you are adding. If you can't fix your mistake, you can push the (C) key once or twice until the screen shows 0. Then start over.

3. Your total should be 1,131. You can use the total to find the average. Just divide by the number of months in the year.

Rainfall	
Month	**Rain (mm)**
Jan.	214
Feb.	138
Mar.	98
Apr.	157
May	84
June	41
July	5
Aug.	23
Sept.	48
Oct.	75
Nov.	140
Dec.	108

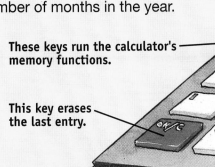

These keys run the calculator's memory functions.

This key erases the last entry.

Using a Balance

A balance is used to measure mass. Mass is the amount of matter in an object. Place the object to be massed in the left pan. Place standard masses in the right pan.

Measure the Mass of an Orange

1. Check that the empty pans are balanced, or level with each other. The pointer at the base should be on the middle mark. If it needs to be adjusted, move the slider on the back of the balance a little to the left or right.

2. Place an orange on the left pan. Notice that the pointer moves and that the pans are no longer level with each other. Then add standard masses, one at a time, to the right pan. When the pointer is at the middle mark again, the pans are balanced. Each pan holds the same amount of mass.

3. Each standard mass is marked to show the number of grams it contains. Add the number of grams marked on the masses in the pan. The total is the mass in grams of the orange.

Using a Spring Scale

A spring scale is used to measure force.
You can use a spring scale to find the weight
of an object in newtons. You can also use
the scale to measure other forces.

Measure the Weight of an Object

1. Place the object in a net bag, and
hang it from the hook on the bottom of
the spring scale. Or, if possible, hang the
object directly from the hook.

2. Slowly lift the scale by the top hook.
Be sure the object to be weighed continues to hang from the bottom hook.

3. Wait until the pointer on the face of
the spring scale has stopped moving.
Read the number next to the pointer to
determine the weight of the object in
newtons.

Measure Friction

1. Hook the object to the bottom of the
spring scale. Use a rubber band to con-
nect the spring scale and object if needed.

2. Gently pull the top hook of the scale
parallel to the floor. When the object

starts to move, read the number of newtons next to the pointer on the scale.
This number is the force of friction
between the floor and the object as you
drag the object.

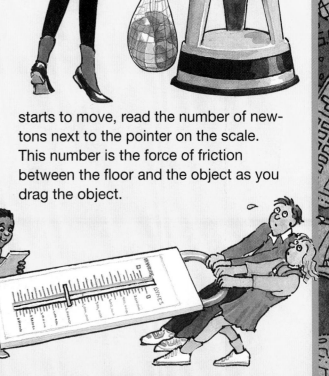

Using a Thermometer

A thermometer is used to measure temperature. When the liquid in the tube of a thermometer gets warmer, it expands and moves farther up the tube. Different units can be used to measure temperature, but scientists usually use the Celsius scale.

Measure the Temperature of a Cold Liquid

1. Half-fill a cup with chilled liquid.

2. Hold the thermometer so that the bulb is in the center of the liquid.

3. Wait until you see the liquid in the tube stop moving. Read the scale line that is closest to the top of the liquid in the tube.

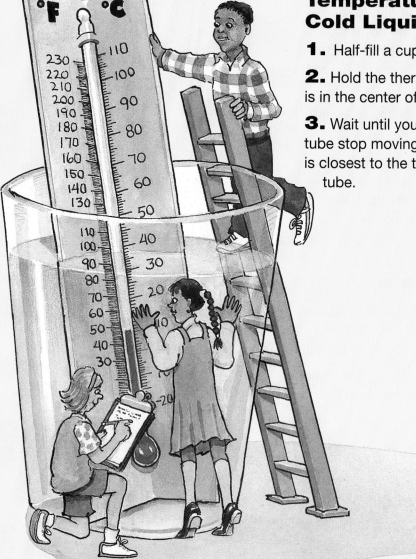

Measuring Volume

A graduated cylinder, a measuring cup, and a beaker are used to measure volume. Volume is the amount of space something takes up. Most of the containers that scientists use to measure volume have a scale marked in milliliters (mL).

Measure the Volume of Juice

1. Pour the juice into a measuring container.

2. Move your head so that your eyes are level with the top of the juice. Read the scale line that is closest to the surface of the juice. If the surface of the juice is curved up on the sides, look at the lowest point of the curve.

3. You can estimate the value between two lines on the scale to obtain a more accurate measurement.

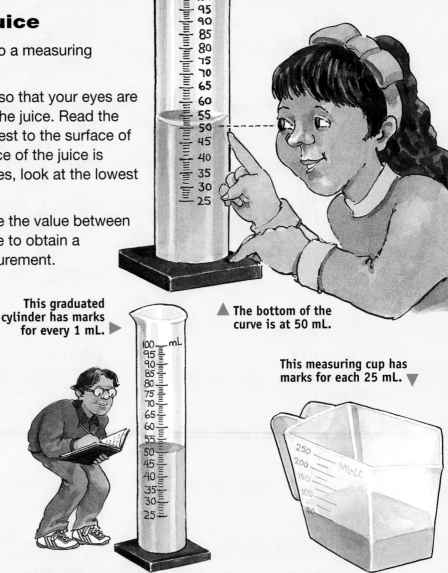

▲ The bottom of the curve is at 50 mL.

This graduated cylinder has marks for every 1 mL. ▶

This beaker has marks for each 25 mL. ▼

This measuring cup has marks for each 25 mL. ▼

Each container above has 50 mL of juice.

MEASUR

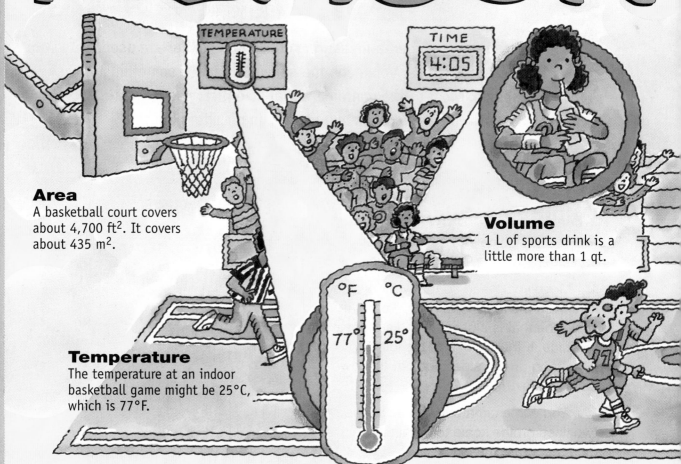

Area
A basketball court covers about 4,700 ft^2. It covers about 435 m^2.

Temperature
The temperature at an indoor basketball game might be 25°C, which is 77°F.

Volume
1 L of sports drink is a little more than 1 qt.

SI Measures

Temperature
Ice melts at 0 degrees Celsius (°C)

Water freezes at 0°C

Water boils at 100°C

Length and Distance
1,000 meters (m) = 1 kilometer (km)

100 centimeters (cm) = 1 m

10 millimeters (mm) = 1 cm

Force
1 newton (N) =
1 kilogram x meter/second/second
(kg x m/s^2)

Volume
1 cubic meter (m^3) = 1 m x 1 m x 1 m

1 cubic centimeter (cm^3) =
1 cm x 1 cm x 1 cm

1 liter (L) = 1,000 milliliters (mL)

1 cm^3 = 1 mL

Area
1 square kilometer (km^2) = 1 km x 1 km

1 hectare = 10,000 m^2

Mass
1,000 grams (g) = 1 kilogram (kg)

1,000 milligrams (mg) = 1 g

EMENTS

Mass and Weight
A basketball has a mass of about 650 g. It weighs about $1\frac{1}{2}$ lb.

Length/ Distance
A basketball rim is about 10 ft high, or a little more than 3 m from the floor.

Rates (SI and English)

km/h = kilometers per hour

m/s = meters per second

mph = miles per hour

English Measures

Volume of Fluids
8 fluid ounces (fl oz) = 1 cup (c)

2 c = 1 pint (pt)

2 pt = 1 quart (qt)

4 qt = 1 gallon (gal)

Temperature
Ice melts at 32 degrees Fahrenheit (°F)

Water freezes at 32°F

Water boils at 212°F

Length and Distance
12 inches (in.) = 1 foot (ft)

3 ft = 1 yard (yd)

5,280 ft = 1 mile (mi)

Weight
16 ounces (oz) = 1 pound (lb)   2,000 pounds = 1 ton (T)

GLOSSARY

Pronunciation Key

Symbol	Key Words
a	cat
ā	ape
ä	cot, car
e	ten, berry
ē	me
i	fit, here
ī	ice, fire
ō	go
ô	fall, for
oi	oil
ōo	look, pull
ōō	tool, rule
ou	out, crowd
u	up
ʉ	fur, shirt
ə	a in ago
	e in agent
	i in pencil
	o in atom
	u in circus
b	bed
d	dog
f	fall

Symbol	Key Words
g	get
h	help
j	jump
k	kiss, call
l	leg
m	meat
n	nose
p	put
r	red
s	see
t	top
v	vat
w	wish
y	yard
z	zebra
ch	chin, arch
ŋ	ring, drink
sh	she, push
th	thin, truth
th	then, father
zh	measure

A heavy stress mark ' is placed after a syllable that gets a heavy, or primary, stress, as in **picture** (pik′chər).

A

abyssal plain (ə bis'əl plān) The broad, flat ocean bottom. (E34) The *abyssal plain* covers nearly half of Earth's surface.

acceleration (ak sel er ā'shən) The rate at which velocity changes over time. (F21) The spacecraft's *acceleration* increased as it soared into the air.

acid (as'id) A compound that turns blue litmus paper to red and forms a salt when it reacts with a base. (C81) *Acids* have a sour taste.

action force The initial force exerted in a force-pair. (F92) When you push against something, you are applying an *action force*.

aftershock A less powerful shock following the principal shock of an earthquake. (B58) Many *aftershocks* shook the ground in the days after the major earthquake.

algae (al'jē) Any of various plantlike protists. (A35) Diatoms and seaweed are kinds of *algae*.

allergy (al'ər jē) An oversensitivity to a specific substance that is harmless to most people, such as pollen, dust, animal hair, or a particular food. (G42) An *allergy* may cause such symptoms as sneezing, itching, or a rash.

alloy (al'oi) A solution of two or more metals. (C59) Bronze is an *alloy* of copper and tin.

antibiotic (an tī bī ät'ik) A substance, produced by microbes or fungi, that can destroy bacteria or stop their growth. Also, a synthetic substance with these properties. (A59) Doctors prescribe *antibiotics* to treat various bacteria-caused diseases.

antibody (an'ti bäd ē) A protein produced in the blood that destroys or weakens bacteria and other pathogens. (A59, G35) *Antibodies* are produced in response to infection.

aquaculture (ak'wə kul chər) The raising of water plants and animals for human use or consumption. (E80) Raising catfish on a catfish "farm" is a form of *aquaculture*.

asexual reproduction Reproduction involving a cell or cells from one parent and resulting in offspring exactly like the parent. (D10) The division of an amoeba into two cells is an example of *asexual reproduction*.

asthenosphere (as then'ə sfir) The layer of Earth below the lithosphere; the upper part of the mantle. (B39) The *asthenosphere* contains hot, partially melted rock with plasticlike properties.

astronomical unit A unit of measurement equal to the distance from Earth to the Sun. (F9) Pluto is 39.3 *astronomical units* (A.U.) from the Sun.

atom The smallest particle of an element that has the chemical properties of that element. (C35) An *atom* of sodium differs from an *atom* of chlorine.

atomic number (ə täm′ik num′bər) The number of protons in the nucleus of an atom of an element. (C73) The *atomic number* of oxygen is 8.

bacteria (bak tir′ē ə) Monerans that feed on dead organic matter or on living things. (A51, G33) Diseases such as pneumonia and tuberculosis are caused by *bacteria*.

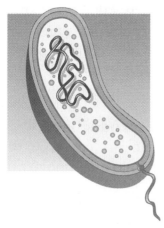

base A compound that turns red litmus paper blue and that forms a salt when it reacts with an acid. (C81) *Bases* have a slippery feel.

behavioral risk factor (bē hāv′yər əl risk fak′tər) A health risk factor that results from a person's choices about his or her lifestyle. (G53) Using drugs or alcohol is a *behavioral risk factor.*

benthos (ben′thäs) All the plants and animals that live on the ocean bottom. (E25) *Benthos* include oysters, crabs, and coral.

blue-green bacteria (bl$\overline{oo}$ grēn bak tir′ē ə) Monerans that contain chlorophyll. (A51) Like plants, *blue-green bacteria* carry out photosynthesis and make their own food.

budding A form of asexual reproduction in which a new individual develops from a bump, or bud, on the body of the parent. (D13) Some one-celled organisms, such as yeast, reproduce by *budding.*

buoyancy (boi′ən sē) The tendency of fluids, like water, to keep objects afloat. (F123) Objects float better in salt water than in fresh water because salt water has greater *buoyancy.*

caldera (kal der′ə) A large circular depression, or basin, at the top of a volcano. (B104) The eruption formed a *caldera* that later became a lake.

cast fossil (kast fäs′əl) A fossil formed when minerals from rock move into and harden within the space left by a decaying organism. (D57) *Cast fossils* of shells can provide information about the animals from which the fossils formed.

cell The basic unit that makes up all living things. (A9) The human body is made up of trillions of *cells.*

cell differentiation (sel dif ər en shē-ā'shən) The development of cells into different and specialized cell types. (A25) Through *cell differentiation*, plant and animal cells develop into tissues.

cell membrane (sel mem'brān) The structure that surrounds and encloses a cell and controls the movement of substances into and out of the cell. (A10) The *cell membrane* shrank when the cell was placed in salt water.

cell respiration (sel res pə rā'shən) The process in cells in which oxygen is used to release stored energy by breaking down sugar molecules. (A19) The process of *cell respiration* provides energy for a cell's activities.

cell theory A theory that states that cells are the basic units of structure and function of all living things. (A10) The *cell theory* states that new cells are produced from existing cells.

cell wall The rigid structure surrounding the cells of plants, monerans, and some protists. (A10) The *cell wall* gives a cell its rigid shape.

chemical bond A force, or link, that holds atoms together in a molecule or in a crystal. (C73) In a water molecule, atoms of hydrogen and oxygen are held together by *chemical bonds*.

chemical change A change in matter that results in new substances with new properties. (C69) A *chemical change* occurs when wood burns and forms gases and ash.

chemical formula A group of symbols and numbers that shows what elements make up a compound. (C40) The *chemical formula* for carbon dioxide is CO_2.

chemical properties Characteristics of matter that describe how it changes when it reacts with other matter. (C34) The ability to burn is a *chemical property* of paper.

chemical symbol One or two letters used to stand for the name of an element. (C36) Ca is the *chemical symbol* for calcium.

chloroplast (klôr'ə plast) A tiny green organelle that contains chlorophyll and is found in plant cells and some protist cells. (A10) The chlorophyll inside a *chloroplast* enables a plant cell to capture solar energy.

cholesterol (kə les'tər ôl) A fatty substance, found in foods, that can lead to clogged blood vessels. (G60) A diet that is too high in *cholesterol* can increase the risk of heart disease.

chromosome (krō'mə sōm) A threadlike structure in the nucleus of a cell; it carries the genes that determine the traits an offspring inherits from its parent or parents. (A10, D22, G12) Most cells in the human body contain 23 pairs of *chromosomes*.

cilia (sil'ē ə) Small, hairlike structures lining the membranes of the respiratory system. (G33) *Cilia* help to filter the air that enters the body.

cinder-cone volcano (sin'dər kōn väl kā'nō) A kind of volcano, usually small and steep-sloped, that is formed from layers of cinders, which are sticky bits of volcanic material. (B88) *Cinder-cone volcanoes* result from explosive eruptions.

communicable disease (kə myōō'ni-kə bəl di zēz) A disease that can be passed from one individual to another. (A58) Bacteria, which are easily passed from organism to organism, are the cause of many *communicable diseases.*

competition The struggle among organisms for available resources. (D77) *Competition* among members of a species is a factor in evolution.

composite-cone volcano (kəm päz'it kōn väl cā'nō) A kind of volcano formed when explosive eruptions of sticky lava alternate with quieter eruptions of volcanic rock bits. (B89) Mount Vesuvius is a *composite-cone volcano* in southern Italy.

compound (käm'pound) A substance made up of two or more elements that are chemically combined. (C34) Water is a *compound* made up of hydrogen and oxygen.

condensation (kän dən sā'shən) The change of state from a gas to a liquid. (C28) The *condensation* of water vapor can form droplets of water on the outside of a cold glass.

continental edge (kän tə nent''l ej) The point at which the continental shelf, which surrounds each continent, begins to angle sharply downward. (E33) Beyond the *continental edge* the ocean increases rapidly in depth.

continental rise The lower portion of the continental slope, extending to the ocean floor. (E33) The *continental rise* usually starts angling down to the ocean floor about a mile beneath the ocean.

continental shelf The sloping shelf of land, consisting of the edges of the continents under the ocean. (E32) The *continental shelf* can extend hundreds of miles out into the ocean.

continental slope The steep clifflike drop from the continental edge to the ocean floor. (E33) The *continental slope* connects the continental shelf with the ocean bottom.

convection (kən vek'shən) The process by which heat energy is transferred through liquids or gases by the movement of particles. (B39) The pie in the oven was heated by *convection.*

convection current The path along which energy is transferred during convection. (B39) Scientists think that *convection currents* in the mantle cause Earth's tectonic plates to move.

convergent boundary (kən vur'jənt boun'də rē) A place where the plates that make up Earth's crust and upper mantle move together. (B40) Layers of rock may bend or break at a *convergent boundary.*

Coriolis effect (kôr ē ō'lis e fekt') The tendency of a body or fluid moving across Earth's surface to have a curving motion due to Earth's rotation. (E56) The *Coriolis effect* causes air and water currents to move to the right in the Northern Hemisphere and to the left in the Southern Hemisphere.

crest The top of a wave. (E65) The *crest* of the wave seemed to tower over the surfer.

crust The thin outer layer of Earth. (B19) Earth's *crust* varies from 5 km to 48 km in thickness.

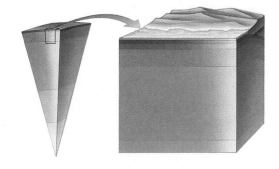

current Great rivers of water moving through the ocean. (E55) The *current* pulled the boat away from shore.

cytoplasm (sīt'ō plaz əm) The watery gel inside a cell. (A11) Various organelles are found inside the *cytoplasm* of a cell.

deceleration (dē sel ər ā'shən) A decrease in speed over time. (F23) Air resistance can cause the *deceleration* of objects.

density The amount of mass in a given volume of matter. (C13) Lead has a greater *density* than aluminum.

desalination (dē sal ə nā'shən) A process for obtaining fresh water from salt water by removing the salt. (E80) A few countries operate *desalination* plants, which obtain fresh water from ocean water.

diatom (dī'ə täm) A microscopic, one-celled alga with a glasslike cell wall. (A35) A single liter of sea water may contain millions of *diatoms.*

dietary fat A nutrient in food that provides energy. (G60) A small amount of *dietary fat* is part of a healthful diet.

diffusion (di fyoo'zhən) The tendency of substances to move from an area of greater concentration to an area of lesser concentration. (A16) Substances can pass in and out of cells by *diffusion.*

divergent boundary (di vur'jənt boun'də rē) A place where the plates that make up Earth's crust and upper mantle move away from one another. (B40) Most *divergent boundaries* are found on the floor of the ocean.

dome mountain A mountain formed when magma lifts Earth's surface, creating a broad dome, or bulge. (B47) Pikes Peak in Colorado is a *dome mountain.*

domesticated (dō mes'ti kāt əd) Tamed and/or bred to serve people's purposes. (D70) People breed *domesticated* animals such as horses for transportation and other uses.

dominant gene (däm'ə nənt jēn) A gene that has control over how a trait is expressed. (G14) A *dominant gene* will be expressed when paired with a recessive gene.

dominant trait (däm'ə nənt trāt) A trait that if inherited, will be expressed. (D45) Gregor Mendel found that tallness was a *dominant trait* in pea plants.

drag A force that resists forward motion through a fluid; it operates in the direction opposite to thrust. (F111) The air causes *drag* on an airplane.

earthquake A shaking or movement of Earth's surface, caused by the release of stored energy along a fault. (B58) Many *earthquakes* occur near the boundaries between tectonic plates.

egg A female sex cell. (G9) In sexual reproduction an *egg* is fertilized by a sperm.

electron (ē lek'trän) A negatively charged particle in an atom. (C71) The number of *electrons* in an atom usually equals the number of protons.

element (el'ə mənt) A substance that cannot be broken down into any other substance by ordinary chemical means. (C34) Oxygen, hydrogen, copper, iron, and carbon are *elements.*

embryo (em'brē ō) An early stage in the development of an organism. (G10) A fertilized egg develops into an *embryo.*

endangered species A species of animal or plant whose number has become so small that the species is in danger of becoming extinct. (D25) The rhinoceros has become an *endangered species* because poachers slaughter the animals for their horns.

endocrine gland (en'dō krin gland) A gland that produces hormones and releases them directly into the bloodstream. (G22) The thyroid and the pituitary are *endocrine glands.*

environmental risk factor A health risk factor that results from a person's environment. (G53) Breathing smoke from other people's cigarettes is an *environmental risk factor.*

epicenter (ep'i sent ər) The point on Earth's surface directly above an earthquake's point of origin. (B65) The *epicenter* of the earthquake was 2 km north of the city.

era (er'ə) One of the major divisions of geologic time. (D59) Many kinds of mammals developed during the Cenozoic *Era.*

ethanol (eth'ə nôl) A kind of alcohol used to make medicines, food products, and various other items. (A42) *Ethanol* is a flammable liquid.

evaporation (ē vap ə rā'shən) The change of state from a liquid to a gas. (C27) Heat from the Sun caused the *evaporation* of the water.

evolution (ev ə lo̅o̅'shən) The idea that all living things are descended from earlier forms of life, with new species developing over time. (D58) According to the theory of *evolution*, the plants and animals alive today descended from organisms that lived millions of years ago.

extinct (ek stiŋkt') With reference to species, no longer in existence. (D25) Dinosaurs are *extinct.*

extinction (ek stiŋk'shən) The disappearance of species from Earth. (D62) Scientists do not agree about what caused the *extinction* of the dinosaurs.

fault A break in rock along which rock slabs have moved. (B65) The shifting of Earth's tectonic plates can produce a *fault*, along which earthquakes may occur.

fault-block mountain A mountain formed when masses of rock move up or down along a fault. (B47) Mountains in the Great Rift Valley of Africa are *fault-block mountains.*

fermentation (fʉr mən tā'shən) A chemical change in which an organism breaks down sugar to produce carbon dioxide and alcohol or lactic acid. (A19, A42) The chemist used yeast to cause *fermentation* in the sugary liquid.

fertilization (fʉr tə li zā'shən) The process by which a sperm and an egg unite to form a cell that will develop into a new individual. (D24, G9) In humans, *fertilization* produces a cell containing 46 chromosomes, half from the female and half from the male.

fetus (fēt′əs) A stage in the development of an organism that follows the embryo stage. (G10) After about eight weeks, a human embryo is called a *fetus.*

first law of motion The concept that objects at rest tend to remain at rest and objects in motion tend to remain in motion, traveling at a constant speed and in the same direction. (F59) According to the *first law of motion,* a stationary object will stay in place unless some force makes it move.

fission (fish′ən) A method of asexual reproduction in which a parent cell divides to form two new cells. (A51, D10) Many one-celled organisms, such as amoebas, reproduce by *fission.*

focus (fō′kəs) The point, or place, at which an earthquake begins. (B65) The *focus* of the earthquake was about 20 km beneath Earth's surface.

folded mountain A mountain formed when two tectonic plates collide. (B45) The Alps and the Himalayas are *folded mountains.*

food pyramid A model showing the relative amounts of different kinds of food a person should eat each day for a healthful diet. (G59) Grains, including breads, cereals, rice, and pasta, make up the base of the *food pyramid.*

force A push or a pull. (F33, F65) The *force* of friction caused the rolling wagon to slow and then stop.

fossil (fäs′əl) The remains or traces of a living thing, usually preserved in rock. (D56) *Fossils* are usually found in sedimentary rock.

freezing The change of state from a liquid to a solid. (C28) The *freezing* of water occurs at 0°C.

friction (frik′shən) The rubbing of one thing against another. The force of friction resists motion between two surfaces that are in contact with each other. (F73) *Friction* keeps a car's tires from slipping off the road.

fungus (fuŋ′gəs) Any of a large group of organisms that feed on dead organisms or that are parasitic. (A43, G40) A mushroom is a *fungus.*

gene (jēn) One of the units that make up a chromosome; genes determine the traits an offspring inherits from its parent or parents. (D35, G13) Half of your *genes* come from your mother, and half come from your father.

gene splicing (jēn splīs′iŋ) A process by which genes are manipulated to alter the function or nature of an organism, usually by being transferred from one organism to another. (D48) Through *gene splicing*, scientists have transferred a gene for making insulin from one organism to another.

genetic engineering (jə net′ik en jə-nir′iŋ) The process by which genes are manipulated to bring about biological change in species. (D47) Using *genetic engineering* techniques, scientists have successfully combined DNA from different organisms.

gravity (grav′i tē) The force that pulls objects toward Earth; also, the attractive force exerted by a body or object on other bodies or objects. (F33) *Gravity* causes a ball to fall to the ground after it is thrown into the air.

health risk factor An action or condition that increases the probability of getting a disease or becoming injured. (G52) Smoking cigarettes and living in an area with *severe water pollution are* two *health risk factors.*

heat Energy that flows from warmer to cooler regions of matter. (C26) *Heat* can cause matter to change from one state to another.

hereditary risk factor A health risk factor that is passed on through genes from parent to child. (G52) A family history of heart disease is a *hereditary risk factor.*

hormone (hôr′mōn) A chemical substance that acts as a messenger, causing a change in organs and tissues in the body. (G23) Growth *hormones* are released by the pituitary gland.

hot spot A place deep within Earth's mantle that is extremely hot and contains a chamber of magma. (B102) Magma rising from a *hot spot* can break through Earth's crust to form a volcano.

immune system (im myo͞on′ sis′təm) The body's system that defends the body against pathogens. (A59, G33) The *immune system* produces antibodies to fight disease.

immunity (im myo͞on′i tē) The body's resistance to a disease or infection. (G35) Polio vaccine gives people *immunity* to the disease.

incomplete dominance (in kəm-plēt′ däm′ə nəns) The expression of both genes (traits) in a pair, producing a blended effect. (D46) A plant with pink flowers, produced by crossing a plant having red flowers with a plant having white flowers, is an example of *incomplete dominance.*

indicator (in′di kāt ər) A substance that changes color when mixed with an acid or a base. (C81) Paper treated with an *indicator* is used to test whether a compound is an acid or a base.

inertia (in ʉr′shə) The tendency of matter to remain at rest if at rest, or if in motion, to remain in motion in the same direction. (F59) *Inertia* results in passengers in a car moving forward when the driver applies the brakes.

inflammation (in flə mā′shən) A defense response by a part of the body, resulting from infection, injury, or irritation and marked by such symptoms as redness, pain, and swelling. (G33) The boy developed an *inflammation* where he had scraped his knee.

inherited trait (in her′it əd trāt) A trait that is passed on from parents to offspring by means of genes. (D34) Eye color is an *inherited trait*.

ion (ī′ən) An electrically charged atom. Ions form when atoms lose or gain electrons. (C73) A negative *ion* is formed when an atom gains electrons.

island arc A chain of volcanoes formed from magma that rises as a result of an oceanic plate sinking into the mantle. (B96) The Philippine Islands are part of an *island arc*.

kinetic energy (ki net′ik en′ər jē) Energy of motion. (C25) A ball rolling down a hill has *kinetic energy*.

lava (lä′və) Magma that flows out onto Earth's surface from a volcano. (B86) Flaming *lava* poured down the sides of the volcanic mountain.

law of conservation of mass The principle that states that matter can neither be created nor destroyed by a chemical or physical change. (C75) According to the *law of conservation of mass*, burning a log will not destroy any of the log's original mass.

law of conservation of momentum The principle that states that momentum can be transferred but cannot be lost. (F86) The *law of conservation of momentum* explains why the momentum resulting from the collision of two objects equals the total momentum of the objects before they collided.

learned trait (lʉrnd trāt) A trait that is acquired through learning or experience. (D36) The ability to speak Spanish is a *learned trait.*

lift The upward force, resulting from differences in air pressure above and below an airplane's wings, that causes the airplane to rise. (F111) Increasing the size of an airplane's wings increases *lift.*

lithosphere (lith'ō sfir) The solid, rocky layer of Earth, including the crust and top part of the mantle. (B38) The *lithosphere* is about 100 km thick.

magma (mag'mə) The hot, molten rock deep inside Earth. (B86) The *magma* rose through the volcano.

magnetic field (mag net'ik fēld) The space around a magnet within which the force of the magnet is exerted. (B28) The magnet attracted all the iron filings within its *magnetic field.*

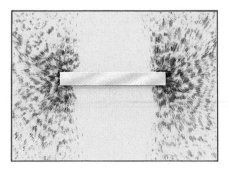

magnetic reversal (mag net'ik ri-vʉr'səl) The switching or changing of Earth's magnetic poles such that the north magnetic pole becomes located at the south magnetic pole's position and vice versa. (B28) Scientists have found evidence of *magnetic reversals* in layers of rock along the ocean floor.

magnitude (mag'nə tōod) The force or strength of an earthquake. (B59) *Magnitude* is a measure of the amount of energy released by an earthquake.

mantle The middle layer of Earth. (B19) The *mantle* is the thick layer of rock between the crust and the core.

mass The amount of matter in an object. (C10, F33) A large rock has more *mass* than a pebble.

matter Anything that has mass and takes up space. (C10) Rocks, water, and air are three kinds of *matter.*

meiosis (mī ō'sis) The process of cell division by which the number of chromosomes in sex cells is reduced to half the number in body cells. (D22) Because of *meiosis*, a sex cell in a human has only 23 chromosomes instead of 46.

melting The change of state from a solid to a liquid. (C27) The *melting* of the icicles began after sunrise.

menstrual cycle (men'strəl sī'kəl) A cycle of approximately 28 days during which an egg is released by the ovary and, if not fertilized, leaves the body with other tissue and blood. (G24) The *menstrual cycle* begins when a girl reaches puberty.

metric system A system of measurement based on a few defined units (such as the meter) and in which larger and smaller units are related by powers of 10. (F11) In the *metric system*, a centimeter is 10 times longer than a millimeter.

microorganism (mī krō ôr'gən iz- əm) An organism too small to be seen except with the aid of a microscope. (G40) Bacteria are *microorganisms*.

mid-ocean ridge A chain of mountains under the ocean. (B22, E34) The *mid-ocean ridge* extends almost 60,000 km.

mitochondria (mīt ō kän'drē ə) Cell organelles in which energy is released from food. (A11) The more *mitochondria* a cell has, the more energy it can release from food.

mitosis (mī tō'sis) The process in which one cell divides to form two identical new cells. (A23) The new cells formed by *mitosis* have the same number of chromosomes as the parent cell.

mixture A combination of two or more substances that can be separated by physical means. (C34) This jar contains a *mixture* of colored beads.

model Something used or made to represent an object or an idea. (C71) The plastic *model* showed the structure of the heart.

mold fossil (mōld fäs'əl) A fossil consisting of a hollowed space in the shape of an organism or one of its parts. (D56) Sediments collecting around a dead organism may lead to the formation of a *mold fossil* of the organism.

molecule (mäl'i kyōōl) A particle made up of a group of atoms that are chemically bonded. (C39) A *molecule* of water contains three atoms.

momentum (mō men'təm) A property of a moving object, calculated by multiplying the object's mass by its velocity. (F85) The train gathered *momentum* as its speed increased.

moneran (män'ər an) Any of mostly one-celled organisms in which the cell does not have a nucleus. (A50) Bacteria are *monerans*.

mucus (myōō'kəs) A thick, sticky fluid that lines the membranes of the respiratory system. (G33) *Mucus* helps trap particles that you breathe in.

multicellular (mul ti sel'yōō lər) Made up of more than one cell. (A33) Some protists are *multicellular*.

mutation (myo͞o tā'shən) A change in a gene that can result in a new characteristic, or trait. (D76) Certain *mutations* have helped species survive in their environment.

natural selection (nach'ər əl sə-lek'shən) The process by which those living things that have characteristics adapting them to their environment tend to live longest and produce the most offspring, passing on these favorable characteristics to their offspring. (D75) *Natural selection* helps explain why certain characteristics become common while others die out.

neap tide (nēp tīd) The tide occurring at the first and third quarters of the Moon, when the difference in level between high and low tide is smallest. (E71) *Neap tides* occur at two times during a month.

nekton (nek'tän) All the free-swimming animals that live in the ocean. (E25) *Nekton* include such animals as fish, octopuses, and whales.

neutralization (no͞o trəl ī zā'shən) The reaction between an acid and a base. (C83) *Neutralization* produces water and a salt.

neutron (no͞o'trän) A particle in the nucleus of an atom that has no electric charge. (C71) The mass of a *neutron* is about equal to that of a proton.

newton (no͞o'tən) A unit used to measure force. (F66) A *newton* is the force needed to accelerate a one-kilogram object by one meter per second every second.

nuclear fission (no͞o'klē ər fish'ən) The splitting of the nucleus of an atom, releasing great amounts of energy. (C77) Bombarding a nucleus with a neutron can cause *nuclear fission*.

nuclear membrane The structure that surrounds and encloses the nucleus and controls what substances move into and out of the nucleus. (A11) The *nuclear membrane* appears to be solid, but it actually has tiny holes through which materials can pass.

nucleus (no͞o'klē əs) 1. The dense, central part of an atom. (C71) The *nucleus* contains nearly all of an atom's mass. 2. The control center of a cell. (A11) The *nucleus* contains the cell's genetic information.

obese (ō bēs') More than 20 percent over normal body weight. (G60) *Obese* people have more health problems than people of normal weight.

organ A part of an multicellular organism made up of a group of tissues that work together to perform a certain function. (A26) The heart and the lungs are *organs* of the human body.

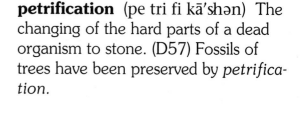

organ system A group of organs that work together to perform one or more functions. (A26) The stomach and the intestines are part of the *organ system* that digests food.

osmosis (äs mō′sis) The diffusion of water through a membrane. (A16) *Osmosis* maintains the balance of water inside and outside a cell.

— **P** —

paleontologist) (pā lē ən täl′ə jist) A scientist who studies fossils. (D58) A team of *paleontologists* discovered the remains of a dinosaur.

Pangaea (pan jē′ə) A supercontinent that existed about 200 million years ago. (B9) *Pangaea* broke apart into several continents.

pathogen (path′ə jən) A microorganism that can cause a disease. (G40) A virus is a *pathogen*.

period 1. A division of geologic time that is a subdivision of an era. (D59) The Jurassic *Period* is part of the Mesozoic Era. 2. The interval of time between two successive wave crests. (E65) The *period* for the ocean waves was about ten seconds.

petrification (pe tri fi kā′shən) The changing of the hard parts of a dead organism to stone. (D57) Fossils of trees have been preserved by *petrification*.

photosynthesis (fōt ō sin′thə sis) The process by which green plants and other producers use light energy to make food. (A18, E24) In *photosynthesis*, plant cells use light energy to make glucose from carbon dioxide and water.

physical change A change in size, shape, or state of matter, with no new kind of matter being formed. (C68) The freezing of water into ice cubes is an example of a *physical change*.

physical properties (fiz′i kəl präp′ər tēz) Characteristics of matter that can be measured or detected by the senses. (C34) Color is a *physical property* of minerals.

phytoplankton (fīt ō plaŋk′tən) Any of the usually microscopic plantlike protists that live near the surface of the ocean. (E11) *Phytoplankton* drift with the ocean currents.

plankton (plaŋk′tən) Organisms, generally microscopic in size, that float or drift in the ocean. (A35, E11) *Plankton* is a source of food for fish.

plate One of the slabs that make up Earth's crust and upper mantle; also called *tectonic plate*. (B19) Some of Earth's *plates* carry continents.

plate boundary A place where the plates that make up Earth's crust and upper mantle either move together or apart or else move past one another. (B20, B40) Earthquakes occur along *plate boundaries.*

pollution The contamination of the environment with waste materials or other unwanted substances. (E91) Dangerous chemicals dumped into the ocean are one source of *pollution.*

polymer (päl'ə mər) A compound consisting of large molecules formed from many smaller, linked molecules. (C92) Proteins are *polymers.*

protist (prōt'ist) Any of a large group of mostly single-celled, microscopic organisms. (A33) Amoebas and algae are *protists.*

proton (prō'tän) A positively charged particle found in the nucleus of an atom. (C71) The atomic number of an atom equals the number of *protons* in the atom's nucleus.

protozoan (prō tō zō'ən) Protists that have animal-like traits. (A34, G40) A paramecium is a *protozoan.*

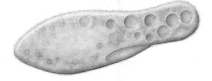

puberty (pyōō'bər tē) The state of physical development when a person becomes capable of producing offspring. (G22) Girls generally reach *puberty* earlier than boys.

radioactive element (rā dē ō ak'tiv el'ə mənt) An element made up of atoms whose nuclei break down, or decay, into nuclei of other atoms. (C76) As the nucleus of a *radioactive element* decays, energy is released.

reaction force The force exerted in response to an action force. (F92) A *reaction force* is equal in strength to an action force but opposite in direction.

recessive gene (ri ses'iv jēn) A gene that is able to control how a trait is expressed only when paired with another recessive gene. (G14) A *recessive gene* will not be expressed when paired with a dominant gene.

recessive trait (ri ses'iv trāt) A trait that will be hidden if paired with a dominant trait. (D45) In his experiments with pea plants, Gregor Mendel learned that shortness was a *recessive trait.*

reproduction The process by which organisms produce more of their own kind. (D10) *Reproduction* ensures the survival of the species.

Richter scale (rik'tər skāl) A scale of numbers by which the magnitude of earthquakes is measured. (B59) Each increase of 1.0 on the *Richter scale* represents an increase of 30 times in the energy released by an earthquake.

rifting (rift′iŋ) The process by which magma rises to fill the gap between two plates that are moving apart. (B108) *Rifting* in eastern Africa may split the continent into two parts.

salinity (sə lin′ə tē) The total amount of dissolved salts in ocean water. (E9) The *salinity* of the ocean varies in different parts of the world.

salt A compound that can be formed when an acid reacts with a base. (C83) When vinegar and baking soda interact, they produce a *salt*.

saprophyte (sap′rə fīt) An organism that lives on dead or decaying matter. (A44) Molds are *saprophytes*.

sea-floor spreading The process by which new ocean floor is continually being formed as magma rises to the surface and hardens into rock. (B30) *Sea-floor spreading* occurs as magma fills the space between separating plates.

seamount (sē′mount) An underwater mountain that formed from a volcano. (E34) Thousands of *seamounts* rise from the floor of the Pacific.

second law of motion The concept that an object's acceleration is related to the strength of the force acting on it and on the object's mass. (F65) A gust of wind blowing an open umbrella out of your hands illustrates the *second law of motion*.

seismograph (sīz′mə graf) An instrument that records the intensity, duration, and nature of earthquake waves. (B74) Scientists use information from *seismographs* to determine the location of earthquakes.

seismometer (sīz mäm′ə tər) An instrument that detects and records Earth's movements. (B98) Data from the *seismometer* suggested that a volcanic eruption might soon occur.

selective breeding Breeding of living things to produce offspring with certain desired characteristics. (D70) People have used *selective breeding* to produce domesticated animals.

sex cell A female or male reproductive cell; an egg cell or sperm cell. (D22) Reproduction can occur when *sex cells* unite.

sexual reproduction Reproduction that involves the joining of a male sex cell and a female sex cell. (D22, G9) Most animals and plants produce offspring through *sexual reproduction*.

shield volcano A kind of volcano that is large and gently sloped and that is formed when lava flows quietly from a crack in the Earth's crust. (B89) Mauna Loa, a *shield volcano* in Hawaii, is the largest volcano on Earth.

solute (säl′y$\overline{oo}$t) The material present in the smaller amount in a solution; the substance dissolved in a solution. (C57) If you dissolve sugar in water, sugar is the *solute.*

solution A mixture in which the different particles are spread evenly throughout the mixture. (C57) Dissolving salt in water makes a *solution.*

solvent (säl′vənt) The material present in the greater amount in a solution; the substance in a solution, usually a liquid, that dissolves another substance. (C57) If you mix sugar and water, water is the *solvent.*

speed The distance traveled in a certain amount of time; rate of movement. (F16) The truck was moving at a *speed* of 40 mph.

sperm (spurm) A male sex cell. (G9) A *sperm* combines with an egg during fertilization.

spore A reproductive cell that can develop into a new organism. (A43) Ferns and mushrooms produce *spores.*

spring tide A tide occurring at or just after the new moon and full moon; usually the highest tide of the month. (E71) At the time of a *spring tide,* both the Sun and the Moon are in line with Earth.

state of matter Any of the three forms that matter may take: solid, liquid, or gas. (C20) Water's *state of matter* depends on its temperature.

substance Matter of a particular kind, or chemical makeup. (C34) Elements and compounds are *substances.*

symbiosis (sim bī ō′sis) A relationship between two organisms in which at least one organism benefits. (A61) Some fungi and algae grow together in *symbiosis.*

tectonic plate *See* plate.

temperature A measure of the average kinetic energy of the particles in matter. (C26) Water *temperature* rises as the motion of water molecules increases.

theory of continental drift A theory that states that the continents formed a single land mass at one time in the past and have drifted over time to their present positions. (B10) The idea of *continental drift* was first suggested by Alfred Wegener.

theory of plate tectonics The theory that Earth's lithosphere is broken into enormous slabs, or plates, that are in motion. (B19, B41) Scientists use the *theory of plate tectonics* to explain how Earth's continents drift.

third law of motion The concept that for every action force there is an equal and opposite reaction force. (F92) When you watch someone's feet bouncing off a trampoline, you see the *third law of motion* at work.

thrust (thrust) The push or driving force that causes an airplane, rocket, or other object to move forward. (F110) *Thrust* can be produced by a spinning propeller or by a jet engine.

tide The daily rise and fall of the surface of the ocean or other large body of water, caused by the gravitational attraction of the Moon and the Sun. (E70) As the *tide* came in, we moved our blanket back from the water's edge.

tissue A group of similar, specialized cells working together to carry out the same function. (A25) Muscle *tissue* contains cells that contract.

toxin (täks'in) A poison produced by an organism. (A58) *Toxins* produced by bacteria can cause serious illness.

trade wind A prevailing wind that blows from east to west on either side of the equator. (E56) South of the equator, the *trade wind* comes from the southeast.

transform-fault boundary (transfôrm fôlt boun'də rē) A place where the plates that make up Earth's crust and upper mantle move past one another. (B41) Movement occurring at a *transform-fault boundary* may cause cracks to form in Earth's rocks.

tsunami (tso͞o nä'mē) A large and powerful ocean wave usually caused by an underwater earthquake. (B76) A *tsunami* can cause great destruction if it strikes a land area.

turbidity current (tʉr bid'i tē kʉr'ənt) A current of water carrying large amounts of sediment. (E38, E61) *Turbidity currents* may cause sediment to build up in some places.

upper mantle (up'ər man'təl) The outermost part of the mantle. (B20) Earth's plates consist of a thin layer of crust lying over the *upper mantle*.

upwelling The rising of deep water to the surface that occurs when winds move surface water. (E60) *Upwelling* brings pieces of shells and dead organisms up from the ocean floor.

vaccine (vak sēn′) A preparation of dead or weakened bacteria or viruses that produces immunity to a disease. (A59, G35) The *vaccine* for smallpox has eliminated that disease.

vacuole (vak′yo͞o ōl) A structure in the cytoplasm in which food and other substances are stored. (A11) A *vacuole* in a plant cell is often quite large.

vegetative propagation (vej ə tāt′iv präp ə gā′shən) A form of asexual reproduction in which a new plant develops from a part of a parent plant. (D15) Using a cutting taken from a houseplant to grow a new plant is a method of *vegetative propagation*.

velocity (və läs′ə tē) The rate of motion in a particular direction. (F21) The *velocity* was northwest at 880 km/h.

virus (vī′rəs) A tiny disease-causing life form consisting of genetic material wrapped inside a capsule of protein. (A52, G40) *Viruses* cause such diseases as AIDS, chickenpox, and rabies.

volcano An opening in Earth's crust through which hot gases, rock fragments, and molten rock erupt. (B48, B86) Lava flowed out of the *volcano*.

volume (väl′yo͞om) The amount of space that matter takes up. (C11) A large fuel tank holds a greater *volume* of gasoline than a small tank.

wave The up-and-down movement of the surface of water, caused by the wind. (E65) Ocean *waves* crashed against the shoreline.

wavelength The distance between the crests of two successive waves. (E65) At the height of the storm, the waves had a *wavelength* of 10 m.

weight A measure of the force of gravity on an object. (F33) The *weight* of this package is five pounds.

westerly (wes′tər lē) A prevailing wind that blows from west to east. (E56) Ships that sailed from North America to Europe were aided by the power of the *westerlies*.

zooplankton (zō ō plaŋk′tən) Any of the tiny animal-like organisms that live near the surface of the ocean. (E11) Zooplankton float in the sea.

zygote (zī′gōt) A fertilized egg cell. (D24, G10) A zygote develops into an embryo by means of cell division.

INDEX

* **Activity**

CREDITS

Cover: *Design, Art Direction, and Production:* Design Five, NYC; *Photography:* Jade Albert; *Photography Production:* Picture It Corporation; *Illustration:* Marti Shohet. **TOC:** Terry Boles, Barbara Cousins, Bob Radigan, Nadine Sokol, John Youssi.

ILLUSTRATORS

UNIT 6A Opener: Lane Yerkes. **Chapter A1:** Keith Kasnot: 22, 23; Briar Lee Mitchell: 26; Michael Kress-Russick: 17, 26; Teri McDermott: 10, 11; Walter Stuart: 25; Ray Vella: 18, 19. **Chapter A2:** David Flaherty: 43, 44; Virge Kask: 33; Kirk Moldoff: 37; Yvonne Walston: 39; Lane Yerkes: 28, 29. **Chapter A3:** Barbara Cousins: 50, 51, 53; Eldon Doty: 55; Ken Tiessen: 61, 62.

UNIT 6B Chapter B1: Skip Baker: 22; Dolores Bego: 7, 30; Warren Budd: 19, 20, 31; Eldon Doty: 8, 9; Eureka Cartography: 17, 18, 20, 21; Geo Systems: 12, 13, 14, 15; Dale Glasgow & Assoc.: 10; Brad Gaber: 29; Greg Harris: 26, 27; Bill Morris: 28; Claudia Karabaic Sargent: 11; Ray Smith: 12, 13, 14, 15. **Chapter B2:** Julie Carpenter: 40, 41; Brad Gaber: 38, 39, 40, 41; Eureka Cartography: 41, 43, 51; Ben Perini 49; Bob Swanson: 45, 47, 48; Randy Verougstraete: 49. **Chapter B3:** Dolores Bego: 77; Bob Brugger: 64; Julie Carpenter: 76, 77, 78; Eldon Doty: 56, 57; Eureka Cartography: 55, 59; Patrick Gnan: 79, 80; Greg Harris: 76, 77, 102; Robert Roper: 64, 65, 67, 81; Robert Schuster: 60; Joe Spencer: 75. **Chapter B4:** Stephen Baur: 107; Dolores Bego: 87; Eldon Doty: 93; Eureka Cartography: 90, 101, 102, 110; Dale Glasgow & Assoc.: 105; Greg Harris: 102, 103, 111; Susan Johnson Carlson: 110; Laszlo Kubini: 92, 96; Bob Swanson: 86, 96, 97; John Youssi: 88, 89, 108, 109.

UNIT 6C Chapter C1: Terry Boles: 15; Patrick Gnan: 11; Mark McIntosh: 29; Andy Meyer: 10, 11, 12; Robert Pasternack: 26, 27; Scott Ross: 12, 19, 20, 21. **Chapter C2:** Bob Brugger: 51; Bill Fox: 34; Adam Mathews: 58; Bob Radigan: 57; Nadine Sokol: 39, 40, 41; Paul Woods: 36, 37, 61. **Chapter C3:** Eldon Doty: 75; Patrick Gnan: 69, 90; George Hardebeck: 76; Steven Mach: 82, 83; Ken Rosenborg: 76, 77; Robert Schuster: 92, 94; Nadine Sokol: 70, 72, 73, 74.

UNIT 6D Chapter D1: Karl Edwards: 10, 11, 12; J.A.K. Graphics: 19, 21, 23; Nina Laden: 10, 11; Kirk Moldoff: 24; Wendy Smith-Griswold: 15, 16, 17. **Chapter D2:** Barbara Cousins: 38, 40, 45; Terry Kovalcik: 37; Sudi McCollum: 33; Teri McDermott: 34, 35, 36, 37, 47; Marjorie Muns: 44, 45; Linda Nye: 42. **Chapter D3:** Drew Brook Cormack: 68, 69; Mona Conner: 74, 75, 76; Richard Courtney: 62; Andy Lendway: 59, 79; Christine Schaar: 66, 67; Raymond Smith: 59, 60, 61; David Uhl: 56, 57; Rosemary Volpe: 70.

UNIT 6E Chapter E1: Terry Boles: 17; Adam Mathews: 17; Bob Radigan: 8, 9, 10, 11; Jim Salvati: 24, 25; Robert Schuster: 11. **Chapter E2:** Barbara Hoopes Ambler: 43; Adam Mathews: 38; Joe McDermott: 32, 33, 49; Steven Nau: 36, 37, 38, 39; Jon Prud' Homme: 36; Bob Radigan: 44, 45; Jeff Seaver: 39. **Chapter E3:** Greg Harris: 65, 73; Jeffery Hitch: 56, 59; Catherine Leary: 65, 66; Adam Mathews: 58, 59, 60, 61; Steven Nau: 62, 63; Jon Prud' Homme: 70, 71; Peter Spacek: 55, 56, 57; Bob Radigan: 92, 93; Gary Torrisi: 84, 85. **Chapter E4:** Eldon Doty: 82, 83; Bob Radigan: E92, E93; Michael Sloan: 80; Dean St. Clair: 91, 92, 93, 94, 95; Gary Torrisi: 84, 85, 86.

UNIT 6F Opener: Ron Fleming **Chapter F1:** Terry Boles: 8, 9, 10; Art Cumings: 24; David Klug: 26; A. J. Miller: 14; Jeffrey Oh: 16, 17; Linda Richards: 25. **Chapter F2:** Terry Boles: 32, 33, 35; Eldon Doty: 38; Don Dixon: 47; Larry Jost: 48, 49; Rebecca Merrilees: 43; Lois Leonard Stock: 46, 47. **Chapter F3:** Terry Boles: 65; Ron Fleming: 52, 53; Dale Glasgow & Assoc.: 68, 69, 77; Jeffery Lynch: 60, 61; Linda Richards: 73, 74, 75, 76; Scott Ross: 58, 59; Michael Sloan: 55, 56, 57. **Chapter F4:** Larry Jost: 95; Bob Novak: 93, Sergio Roffo: 84; Ron Young: 82, 83. **Chapter F5:** Terry Boles: 106, 107, 117; Julie Carpenter: 109; Bob Novak 110, 111, 124; Pete Spacek: 123, 124, 125, 126.

UNIT 6G Opener: Iskra Johnson. **Chapter G1:** Anatoly Chernistov: 22, 23; Iskra Johnson: 4, 5; Claude Martinot: 12, 13, 14, 15; Briar Lee Mitchell: 7; Mary Ellen Niates: 9, 10, 11, 17; Julie Peterson: 25, 26; Stephen Schudlich: 9, 10, 11, 16; Matt Straub: 20, 21; Kate Sweeney: 13, 14, 27. **Chapter G2:** Barbara Cousins: 40, 41; David Flaherty: 32; Marcia Hartsock: 46; Jackie Heda: 32, 33, 34, 35, 47; Briar Lee Mitchell: 42, 43; Leonid Mysakov: 36. **Chapter G3:** Mark Bender: 51, 52, 53; Glasgow & Assoc.: 57; Steven Stankiewicz: 54, 55; Rod Thomas: 59, 60, 61, 62, 63; Beth Anne Willert: 61.

Glossary: Warren Budd and Assoc., Barbara Cousins, Brad Gaber, Patrick Gnan, Verlin Miller, Bob Swanson, David Uhl, John Youssi.

Handbook: Kathleen Dunne, Laurie Hamilton, Catherine Leary, Andy Meyer

Unit A Opener 1–3: © M.I. Walker/Science Source/Photo Researchers. 2: *l.* Grant Heilman Photography. **Chapter 1** 4–5: *bkgd.* David M. Phillips/Visuals Unlimited; *inset* Richard Hutchings for SBG. 6: Ken Karp for SBG. 7: *t.* Ken Karp for SBG; *b.l.* Ken Karp for SBG; *b.r.* © Nursidsany et Perennou/Photo Researchers, Inc. 8: Ken Karp for SBG. 10: © Biophoto Associates/Science Source/Photo Researchers, Inc. 12: *t.* The Science Museum, London/Science & Society Picture Library; *b.* The Science Museum/Science & Society Picture Library. 13: *b.* © Photo Researchers, Inc. 14–16: Ken Karp for SBG. 18: Ruth Dixon/Stock Boston. 19: PhotoEdit. 20: Ken Karp for SBG. 21: Carolina